·

Coming soon from Paul Figueroa

Book three in the Your Life is Calling series:

The Journey to Meaning

Personal workbooks for the Your Life is Calling series:

The Journey Home
The Journey to Meaning
The Journey to Purpose

A book on Workplace Bullying Prevention

Paul is also available for speaking engagements on these and a myriad of other topics.

See www.PaulFigueroa.com for more information.

The names, details and characters are fiction. This publication is not intended to substitute for the advice of health care professionals.

Cover design by Paul Figueroa

Listen,
Your Life is Calling

The Journey to Purpose

Book Two of the

LISTEN, YOUR LIFE IS CALLING SERIES

by Paul Figueroa

1

The last year had been an intense one for Brian. His mom had come out of the closet, so to speak, his stepdad had passed, he'd become rich and lost it all, and he'd turned down an executive job with a prestigious tech company – the very one that had purchased the one he'd helped create. But wait, there's more… his wife had an emotional affair with his best friend, an old man with a fedora had shown up and started dropping knowledge on him, and he moved to Phoenix, Arizona.

The good news was that Brian had gained a greater sense of himself. He felt more like his true self, more at ease than he'd ever felt before, yet, something was missing. He wasn't sure what, yet. Several questions were nagging at him, too. Questions like:

Why am I here?

What is the reason I'm on the planet?

What's the one thing I do that no one else can?

The old man had told him, "Each of us has a reason, Brian. A reason we're here, a purpose for being. Find that, find your purpose and your world will change."

Find that and your world will change, Brian thought.

"It already has, old man. It already has."

Brian just hadn't found his "reason" yet.

A smile came to his face as he thought of the friendly "old man in the fedora." He realized that the old man was the exact opposite of what a man his age usually was. This guy was vibrant, alive and loving life. He obviously had found his purpose and he was walking his talk.

"How do you find it?" Brian had asked him once.

"Easy," the old man had said. "You'll know it when you lose all track of time. Have you ever had three minutes that felt like an eternity, or three minutes that flashed by like a second? Look for the latter, that's your clue – when you're in alignment with your purpose, it'll be fun, easy and joyful."

"Okay, I get it I guess. But, how?"

"Well," he laughed. "It's like anything… you go out looking for it," he chuckled and smiled broadly. "That's it for today," he added. "I'm on a schedule."

"But…"

"You got this, Brian. Have faith, trust in yourself." The old man tapped his hat, scooted out of the booth and left whistling that same song. That same song that Brian could almost place all the other times the old man whistled it.

Hmm Hmmm "We ain't got money…" hmmm hmm.

Dang! I almost have it! Brian thought.

The rest of his day went wonderfully. He got his run in and a nice "walk of blankness," as he started to call it. All was right in his world.

Later that afternoon, he was wandering around downtown Phoenix, taking in the day. He was in the business district amidst the tall concrete monoliths and the occasional "shiny" building. It was sunny, warm and beautiful. He found himself at a crosswalk, waiting. The light turned green and with a smile on his face, he took a step off the light beige curb to cross the hot black pavement. To his left, he heard the loud roar of a car engine. Out of the corner of his eye he caught a glimpse of a small red car… the thing was on him instantly. Tires screeched and squealed, the car's engine hit a fever pitch and jerked violently in front of him. The bright red fender flashed, brushing his left pant leg and nearly taking his leg off with it.

Brian jumped back onto the curb, took a deep breath and then finished crossing the street. He took a few more breaths as the car sped off, quickly going through the gears. Rather than get all caught up in what the driver was doing, Brian reflected on things. He began to wonder if he had done something to contribute to this happening.

It's true, the car driver would have been in the wrong by running the red light... Brian was wondering why he was at that place at that exact moment.

You see, Brian had learned to pay attention, to "listen," to be more aware about what his life was telling him. He knew it sometimes spoke to him in ways just like this. Thanks to the "old man," he'd been able to change his life for the better by doing this very thing.

Brian thought about what happened and he realized that he was "spacing out" a bit before the car almost hit him. He was thinking about all the potential "what if's" in his life, and frankly, worrying about things that hadn't even happened yet. He got that during that time, he wasn't completely in his body before the car swooped by.

He started to think about the driver of the car and anger started to swell from within him, he was really working himself up. Just as the anger was turning to rage, he stopped.

Somewhere he had heard, "Underneath anger, more times than not, is fear." Realizing this, the anger dissipated started to dissipate. The fact was, when he thought about the car almost hitting him, underneath it was the fact that he was afraid of getting hit. He was scared by how close it came.

Click.

It suddenly occurred to him that his brain was creating all this "excitement" from an event that was over. The fact was, he was okay. The car didn't really hit him, but he was taking what happened personally. You see, sometimes other people just aren't aware, or they don't care. It's nothing personal, though.

Brian also got that in going back, in replaying and reliving the event, he wasn't doing himself, or his life, any good. He knew that anger, misguided and reacted to, never amounted to much. The event was over. Pure and simple, he was safe, so he needed to let it "be over."

He took a deep breath and snapped back into the here and now.

Brian walked around a bit more, shook off what happened and got back to enjoying the sunshine. He made a promise to himself to worry less and to be even more aware of what his brain was doing.

He allowed himself to feel the presence and depth of the warm desert air. He became aware of the calmness that he felt. There was something about this place. Phoenix felt like home to him, he realized it always had. Years ago, he had he made a stopover on a trip to Florida and he'd noticed it. It flat out felt like home.

You may be wondering, how could he shake of an event like this? After all, he was almost hit by a car. Well, Brian's been practicing and reflecting quite a bit of late. He's noticed that his brain, that fear, wasn't always his friend or ally. He began to see how he actually could master his reactions and his tendencies. In this instance, he had done a fine job.

Thirty minutes later, Brain found himself down by the Diamondback's baseball field, taking in his day. He was back, centered and at peace.

"Find your purpose," he said out loud.

That old man talks in riddles, he thought. *He's never direct.*

What else did he say?

"Find where you lose track of time."

Okay, old man. Okay.

The thing was, Brian just didn't do what other people told him anymore. He'd learned that earlier in the year - doing what others told him didn't get him what he wanted. What did work for him was to go with what he knows, what fits and feels right, and frankly, what the old man had said fit.

He had also learned that you can't figure out questions like this, all his brain would do is get in the way. It was like trying to figure out what a roller coaster ride would feel like without actually being on, or going on, the roller coaster. You can cerebralize it, but it just wasn't the same as "being" in the experience. Thus the term, "You'll know."

Okay, what's next? he wondered.

He knew he loved hanging out with kids. He liked how direct, unfiltered and on the spot they were with what they said. It occurred to him that this was his next step. To explore that. He suddenly flashed to when he was younger, a six year old boy at home, in his bedroom, playing.

Mr. Whiskers, his chubby light brown teddy bear, had an Ace Bandage on it's little left arm.

> "I can fix you," he said to Mr. Whiskers in his soft six year old doctor voice.

> His mom walked in. "Brian, what are you doing?"

> "I'm a Doctor, Mommy. I'm helping kids."

> "No. No you're not," she said with a sharp voice. "Doctors get sued, they suffer from malpractice suits and work all their lives. Do you remember what Jerry said, 'Work hard and a man can achieve anything?'"

> "Yes."

> "Well, you can retire one day. He says that computers are the thing, not doctoring. Besides, you don't really want to help children, do you? You don't want to be a doctor."

> "No Mommy. No, I guess not."

Brian was catapulted back into the present. His heart ached and a tear formed on the outside of his right eye.

"Okay, that's good to know," he said as he exhaled.

The backup of emotions from that event were momentarily caught in his throat. After a few moments, they left, washed away with the tears that were streaming down his cheeks. He wiped them away with his hands.

"Go looking for it," the old man said.

Okay. That's it. The next step.

He smiled. The smile wasn't so much about knowing what his next step was, it was more about a sense of pride about the progress he was making. He liked the man he was becoming, or rather, the man he truly was. He was truly recognizing himself again.

He woke up the next morning, excited to be alive and to discover what his "thing" was, his "purpose" in life.

Then, it happened - his brain kicked in.

"Mini-fears" started to pop up as "micro" thoughts crept in. He started to worry. Even larger thoughts worked their way into his awareness - fear of failure, not being good enough and of looking stupid. A wave of fear began to engulf him. Sweat formed on his face and chest, and a pulse of electricity moved through his body. His stomach started to turn sour and an enormous weight started bearing down upon on him. It was like a seventy-five pound lead blanket had been thrown on top of him. He was sweating profusely now, his stomach was upset and he flat out couldn't move. His thoughts and fears had stopped him cold. He was immobilized, like he had been hit by a semi-truck, left lying inert on the highway with a huge weight on him.

He took a deep breath. He struggled to move. Slowly, with his left hand, he moved the sweat from his forehead and wiped it on his night shirt.

Everything will be okay.

"Everything will be okay," he whispered to himself.

Tears formed, flowed and grew. Moments later, the fear started to subside. He felt off. He felt heavy, slow... wrung out.

He slowly started to move. He got out of bed and went to the bathroom. He flicked on the light, turned on the warm water and splashed it gently onto his face. He looked at himself in the mirror and forced a smile. He took a deep breath and went to his desk in the living room.

He pulled out the chair, sat down and opened a notepad.

What am I afraid of?

He began to write.

> *That I won't have enough money.*
>
> *That people will think I'm odd, that I'm weird.*
>
> *That I'll fail.*
>
> *That I'm stupid.*
>
> *That I won't find my purpose.*
>
> *That this whole thing is a sham.*
>
> *That I should have stayed with Melinda.*

That I should have stayed with Micro Tech.

A knot formed in his stomach. He could feel it as it grew inside him, much like a heavy, wet, three inch wide chunk of lead rope. As it grew, it coiled around itself and laid there, static, not moving. Heavy. Lead, in the pit of his stomach.

This knot was familiar, it had become an uncomfortable friend. He had learned that it was an indicator that something was up. As uncomfortable as it was, it served a purpose for him. It had a reason.

He looked down at the paper. His fears were staring back at him, almost daring him to look.

After a few moments, he discovered several things.

1. His penmanship wasn't that hot when he was afraid.
2. He saw how quickly one fear led to another, and another, and another when he was in this place.
3. All that fear led to second guessing, second guessing choices he knew were right for him, and
4. What he wrote was like a snowball; the more he wrote from that place, the bigger the fears got.

He laughed out loud as he tossed his pen on his desk.

Man, my brain is amazing. Look how quick it went from "A" to "Godzilla!"

He took a deep breath. As he slowly exhaled, he knew what he needed.

Some dead air time. Some "no think" time and a 'walk of blankness."

He found his running gear and got changed. As he focused on lacing and tying his shoes, he realized that the fear was now almost completely gone.

A tear started to form in his left eye and his heart started to warm.

Brian laughed.

What you focus on gets bigger, old man. I get it. I get it!

He hopped into his rig and headed to his favorite workout place. He did his normal stretching routine, warmed up and headed out. It was nice and warm, and the sun was greeting him along with the day. He loved this time for him, he felt grateful and appreciated that he did this for himself.

About twenty minutes in, he felt the urge to stop. He took a few more strides, slowed to a trot and took a deep breath. He looked around and noticed the vista around him, it was gorgeous, breathtaking. He had a sweeping view of downtown Phoenix and he could see pretty much everything. The air was so crisp and warm. As he took a breath, the warmth of the air seemed to revitalize him, like there was energy inside it.

It occurred to him that he was so focused on what he was doing, he hadn't really even noticed the beauty around him. He knew it was there, he just never really looked.

He was up in the "Camelback" area of Phoenix. He was surrounded by beautiful red rock earth, scattered cactus and a crisp dry smell he so enjoyed. He took another few moments and looked around. The houses were spectacular. Most had gated fences and paved drives that lead up to ornate entry ways. They area had such a good feeling to Brian, he started to smile. It was like he knew he would live here someday.

I've always wanted to live up here.

Quickly, he realized that this type of thinking was him not being present… again. He laughed. He remembered hearing from somewhere an idea, it was Eckhart Tolle if he remembered right:

> To observe is one thing. To notice a tree's beauty, its presence, anything really, is one thing. Once you start thinking about how it would look in your yard, where you would put it, well, you're no longer observing, you're no longer present. You're thinking, you're not really seeing… and you're out of the moment.

While all of what he was seeing was true, he realized there was a line –a very thin one that's hard to see most of the time.

He got it. He was no longer really looking at what he was seeing. He was judging it, analyzing it, reaching and applying meaning to it and once he did, he was no longer present and the moment was lost. It struck him that someday he would live here, yet right now, the view, the surroundings and the air was enough.

He was immediately brought back to the moment and felt not only the enormity of the insight, he felt a deeper appreciation and gratitude for his surroundings.

It occurred to him that:

> *My brain's conditioned to set up misery.*
>
> *It seems to never be satisfied with what is.*
>
> *It's always about doing, creating or making something better.*

Interesting

He chuckled, took another breath of the vibrant Phoenix air and resumed his run.

2

Later that day, Brian was puttering around his apartment and remembered he had a friend that was a teacher in the area.

Click.

A smile grew on his face as he remembered her name, Tina. She was a teacher and she worked with second graders at a local grade school. His smile broadened as the idea of volunteering popped in. Later that evening, he gave her a call.

"Hi Tina, it's Brian. How are you?"

"I'm good Brian, it's been a long time. How have you been?"

"Wonderful, really. Thanks for asking. Things couldn't be better," he paused. "Say, I have a question for you."

"Sure. What's up?"

"Would it be possible for me to volunteer with you? I'm discovering what I want to do next, job wise, and I wanted to check out what you do." It struck him how odd the word "job" felt. Right when he said it, it didn't feel right, it felt like drudgery.

"Sure Brian, you bet. That would be fun, I bet you'll be great with the kids. When were you thinking?"

"Would tomorrow work?"

"You are direct," she chuckled. He could hear her smile through the telephone. "Well, we have testing tomorrow, so how about Thursday? Would that work for you?"

"Sure. What time?"

"I'm doing some reading and a lesson from 10:00 to 10:40 in the morning, that would be fun I think."

"Awesome. Thursday at 10:00 a.m. it is. Say, how do I go about this?" he laughed. "I mean, how do I do this? Do I just show up?"

"Pretty much," she laughed. "I'll let Principal Forester know you're coming. Since you're just coming in to observe, it'll be okay to just sign in at the office. If you end up doing more than that, we can go through all the paperwork."

"Deal... wait," he laughed. "Where do you teach? I forgot to ask."

"I'm at Maple Glen Elementary, in Scottsdale," she laughed.

"Thanks, Tina, I'll see you Thursday."

"Sure, Brian, glad to. I'll see you then."

Brian swiped left, ending the call and he sat back in his chair. He was smiling and a sense of being on the right track showed up, too.

Phase one of 'Project discovery of purpose' initiated.

He felt nervous, relaxed and excited, all at the same time.

Odd. I wonder where that nervousness is coming from.

This past year had been, by most accounts, traumatic for Brian. With all the loss he had experienced, most people would have fought it, turned pessimistic and become "doom and gloomy." For Brian, he had realized all the things that happened were serving a purpose in his life. While they seemed unpleasant at the time, looking back, he saw how he'd become a better and much happier person because of them.

The relationship with his wife, Melinda, had pretty much ended. Part of this was because of the emotional affair she had with his best friend, Chuck. Yes, you heard correctly, his best friend. It also was ending because he was realizing he was with her for the wrong reasons. While he still loved her deeply, he knew she wasn't the right fit for him. He knew it, deep down.

Brian realized he needed to clean out that chapter of his life and he knew that something better was coming for him. If he didn't clean it out, if he didn't completely close that door, nothing new could come in. This excited him because parts of his relationship with Melinda were pretty flippin' great! He knew that ending it, getting divorced and finalizing things would leave room for something even better. That was the excitement too, see? If he didn't end it, he'd be blocking the future, prolonging the pain and misery.

He began to remember one of the conversations with the old man, they were talking about decisions. The old man had said, "When one doorway closes, another other opens, Kiddo. If one door isn't closed all the way, well, it's difficult for the other one to open - let alone for you to go through it. Yes, the hallway can be a drag sometimes, but it's worth it. They're worth it. Think of it this way: You can choose to stay, to prolong things and be unsure of yourself, or you can close the door, be in the hallway and be excited about who's coming through the next door. Trust me, I tried not shutting the door all the way once. It wasn't fun."

Even more changes had been afoot for him this last year. Brian had formed a tech company with his ex-best friend, Chuck. Yes, that same "Chuck." He and Chuck had sold the company to Ang & Tanaka Incorporated, and Brian had become a multi-millionaire overnight. He was receiving national attention and he thought he had everything he wanted. His life had been going exactly the way he planned. He was rich, yet it was as if his life was unraveling at the same time.

During that time, there was something that eluded him... it was bugging him really. True, there was a problem with his relationship – he knew that. He was pretty sure it wouldn't work, yet he had this profound empty feeling inside. It was as if a guitar was being played over a deep hole, and the tune sounded flat and off key. Brian's life... really, Brian was out of tune. The good news was that he recognized it, he was aware of it and he was doing something about it.

So, there Brian was, a multi-millionaire and he did the prudent thing, what most all of us would do. He called an old friend of his and invested most all of his money in the stock market and "other vehicles."

Well, I bet you already figured out the next part. The investments turned sour and his friend was, well, shall we say "less than honest." Yup, Brian lost pretty near everything. While he no longer had enough to retire on, his millions were gone, he did have a small amount in savings - a safety net of sorts.

All of these changes would devastate most people. Not Brian. Something inside him knew he would come out of all this okay. Better than okay.

"Everything happens for a reason," the old man had said.

Everything happens for a reason.

That Thursday, he got up a bit early, went for his run and stopped in to his favorite café. Every time he opened the creaky door, he heard the bell chime and remembered the old man.

What was it about him? he wondered.

He had such a way about him, an ease... It was like he always knew things were working out.

Brian started to realize how found he was becoming of him. Not only for the "gifts of knowledge" he'd received, he was glad the old man was in his life.

Brian finished his normal meal of eggs and juice, left a generous tip for his now familiar waitress, Becky, and headed to his rig. He fired it up and was off to his next stop.

He pulled into the Maple Glen Elementary school parking lot a bit before 9:45. He started grinning from ear to ear and he realized he was a bit nervous, too.

Where's that coming from? he wondered.

He parked, hopped out of his rig and headed for the main doors. Right as he opened them, he was met by a familiar smell. It reminded him of his school days growing up, plus, there was a quiet energy about this place. He liked it.

Brian found the main office where he was greeted by a smiling receptionist with a headset.

"Good morning," she said.

"Good morning. I'm looking for Mrs. Hollingsworth's room, I'm volunteering today."

"Sure. She is out the door and two rights, on the right. It's room 121."

She asked him to sign in and put on a volunteer badge. He grabbed the purple piece of square plastic, opened the silver clip and connected it to his red t-shirt. He chuckled, realizing he had gotten rid of most of his long sleeve dress shirts with pockets.

He thanked her and headed out to the hallway. As he took his first right, he immediately noticed the wall to his left. It had a large corkboard area on it, and pegged to it were pictures of all the teachers and staff at the school.

Amazing, he thought. *All these people here helping these kids. Love it.*

He smiled and found his way to Room 121. He was a bit early, so he hung out in the hallway between classrooms. Prominently displayed on the walls were works of art from a couple of the nearby classes. Apparently, they were learning about numbers and how they connected to other things in life.

Johnny, one of the fine young artists, had made a drawing of himself playing baseball. Underneath it he wrote, "Playing baseball is fun. Numbers are too. They keep track of scores. I like playing baseball. I like numbers."

Another youngster, Sheila, had colored herself playing volleyball. "I love volleyball," she wrote. "I count my serves that go in and we count points. Volleyball is fun. Numbers track things. I like chocolate, too. There aren't numbers in it."

He chuckled. *Cute.*

Right then, Tina popped out of the classroom with a big smile on her face.

"Brian, it's so good to see you. It's been so long." She gave him a quick hug. "Come on in, I'll introduce you. You can hang out in the back and soak it in."

"Thanks Tina," he said. Brian was grinning from ear to ear.

They walked through the classroom doorway and she said, "Class, this is Mr. Richardson. He's here to watch what we're up to today." All twenty three children chimed in, "Good morning, Mr. Richardson." Brian smiled broadly, waved and went to the back and took a seat.

It was amazing to him how small everything was. He remembered things being, much, much, MUCH bigger.

Tina started her lesson, reading from a kid's book about bullying. It described how hard of a time this little girl, Shelly, was having at school. The kids were lapping it up.

"Why was that one boy being mean to her?" a youngster asked.

"Well," Tina said, "Sometimes we don't know we're being mean when we are. Have you ever said something you wished you hadn't, but didn't know it when you said it?"

Most of the class nodded.

"Well, part of that is what's going on. A few of the boys and girls being mean to her weren't really aware they were doing it. The one boy, Ned… he was just angry inside."

Several, "Ohhhh's" rang through the room.

"Have you ever been really mad at someone and said or done something mean?" she asked.

Crickets.

"Well, the idea is to learn that you're mad and then stop before you say or do something."

A young boy up front raised his hand.

"Is that why you tell us to be patient with our feelings?"

"Yes, Bobby, that's it exactly. Sometimes, if we just do what we're feeling, well, the choices we make don't turn out the best."

Some more "Ohhhh's" rang through the room.

"Okay, let's open up your spelling book to page seven. It's time to see what you learned from yesterday."

Tina read a list of words and the youngsters spelled them on the sheet. As Brian was watching the class, he realized that this wasn't exactly what he wanted to do. He was smiling, though. He loved the kids. They were amazing, yet he wanted to help them in a different way. He noticed he was drawn more to the behavior part of the day, the bullying, feelings and behavior part. Spelling and reading and the like, well, he could tell his heart wasn't in it.

At the end of their time, he said good bye to the class and thanked Tina.

"You're awesome," he said. "Thanks for letting me come by today."

"You bet, Brian, anytime. What do you think?"

"Well, I love the kids. It just doesn't feel right to me. I loved the bullying part and how you shared to be patient with their feelings, yet my heart just isn't in the reading, writing, and arithmetic part."

"No problem, Brian. I get it. Let me know if you want to come by again. Sometimes it takes a while for it to sink in."

"Thanks, Tina. I appreciate it."

They hugged, and Brian headed back to the school office. He returned the badge, signed out and headed back to his rig. Right as he got in, fear began to engulf him. His brain started to take him into a flat spin and, frankly, it startled him. Worries, fear, anger and the "what if's" were swarming at him like angry bats. He wasn't used to having fear happen so often or so intensely, let alone back to back so soon. He took a deep breath and closed the door to his rig.

Breathe. Breathe. What is going on?

He looked back at his thoughts over the past few hours and realized he had been thinking tiny little "micro thoughts" again, thoughts like: "I'll never find the right career." Also, leaking in was a bit of, "I shouldn't have left Mobile Tech, or Melinda."

He chuckled.

My brain just did an "A to Godzilla" again. Okay, what's the truth? The truth is:

> 1.) *I like that I had the courage to explore this avenue. I'm proud of myself.*
>
> 2.) *Mobile Tech wasn't a fit, nor is Melinda. I know this.*
>
> 3.) *If I hadn't followed my gut - my inner guidance - I wouldn't be available for the right fit, either in a career, or a relationship.*

4.) I like the idea of teaching, maybe in another context, and

5.) I know that even though I don't see it right now, I'm on the right track.

He took another deep breath and let it out.

He remembered a recent conversation he had with the "old man." He'd said, "Brian, our brains don't want us to discover how little we need them. They're afraid that when we do, we'll lay them off." He had a broad grin on his face as he laughed out loud. "You see, they want us to have problems so they have something to do. That's why the solutions to unhooking our brains don't involve doing, they involve being.

"It's funny. Our brains are the very thing that creates the fear, and it wants us to use it to figure it out," he laughed.

"As a matter of fact," he continued, "Oftentimes fears start coming up when we're on the right track, or super close to making positive changes. It's like the brain's trying to put up a fight," he smiled. "It knows it's losing, so it gets scared and pushes really hard, like a bully."

The old man is so smart, he thought. *I wonder how he got that way.*

Brian brought himself back into the present, fired up his rig and went back to his apartment. It was a modest space, yet more than enough for what he was up to. He made himself a smoothie, sat down and vegged for a few minutes, his mind wonderfully blank.

The urge struck him to go down to the local secondhand bookstore. He'd become a big fan of places like this of late. He popped in and found himself in the business section, of all places. He reached out to a book that caught his eye, opened it and started reading midway.

> "How to know you're on the right path. Sometimes, fear gives you information. The mere fact you become afraid can be a sign that a part of you doesn't want to improve. This is also true with your staff. As a manager of people, realize that change can trigger a myriad of responses, most of them disguising the fear underneath."

Interesting, he thought.

He wasn't sure what the managing part had to do with him, yet the other stuff made sense. That explained why he was afraid, lately, too.

Just then, his phone rang. He swiped right and put it to his ear. The earpiece said, "Hi Brian, my name is William, I'm from the Boys and Girls club in Tempe."

"Hi William, how can I help you?"

"Well, Tina, from Maple Glen Elementary… she's a friend of mine. She mentioned that you're discovering what your path is, so to speak, and she said that you're great with kids."

This is odd, he thought.   *Roll with it.*

William continued, "Well, the interesting thing is that we have a position open here at the club. It involves working with young people during the afterschool program. I thought I would see if you're interested."

Your life wants you to succeed. Get out of your own way, Brian.

"Sure," he heard himself say. Literally…. he wasn't sure where the words came from.

"Awesome," said William. "Can you be here today at 2:45? I know it short notice, but we're short staffed."

"Absolutely. I'll see you then." Brian swiped left. He bought the book and headed over to the club. He was met outside by a husky younger man with white hair. He was cordial enough and had tons of energy.

"Hi Brian, I'm William. Glad to meet you."

"Same here," remarked Brian, "Thanks for thinking of me. I'm excited to start."

"Sounds great," William said. "I have some paperwork for you to fill out and sign, you okay with that? It involves a background check, too, so you know."

"No problem," Brian said.

"Great. Either myself of Tammie, she's our program coordinator, will be with you until the paperwork comes back. It should only take a day or two. I hope you understand."

"Absolutely, I get it," said Brain.

William guided him through the two blue, heavy steel doors and walked him back into his office. Right as Brian entered the club, he immediately loved the smell - it reminded him of his high school gym. The thought of shooting hoops again brought a smile to his face.

The office was pretty basic, a couple of old metal desks, a wood table smack in the middle and piles of paper strewn out on a countertop that ran the length of a wall. He glanced at some of the papers on it and it looked like they were working on a newsletter.

"Those are for our monthly newsletter," William mentioned, "We use it to keep people updated, and it's also a way to raise money."

"Awesome," Brian said. "How many people?"

"About 2,300 total. It helps keep things moving for us."

William tossed him a blue polo shirt, "This is your uniform, of sorts," William chuckled. "I'll give you a couple more tomorrow."

Brain thanked him, went to the men's room and changed. 3:15 struck. He headed to the front doors and the wave of kids started coming.

Wow, thought Brian. *This is going to be interesting.* He smiled.

After the first twenty or so kids filed in, a woman in her mid-twenties got out of her light blue Chevy Aveo. Brian took one look at her and his heart flipped in his chest.

What is that!? he wondered. *One more thing to talk to the old man about,* he laughed.

Tammie, the heart flipper, walked up to him and said hello. "You must be Brian," she smiled as they shook hands.

"Yes, it's true," he grinned. "News travels fast."

"Good news does," she said as she smiled at him.

One more heart flip before meeting the sea of kids.

Interesting, he thought.

The "sea of kids" were a wonderful blend of young people ranging from the age of twelve to about seventeen. He noticed how they came in all heights, sizes, shapes and colors. Most of them had their own unique way of being, too.

Some had customized and unique backpacks, others had their own style of dressing and hair, the whole deal. One young man sported a pressed blue and pink plaid shirt and a white bow tie, he made it look good. One young lady had an interesting pair of pants - they were multi colored blue, red and yellow, with rips, tears and multi-colored patches. She wore a flat black shirt with multicolored suspenders and her hair was bright red with black roots. Brian kept smiling, he thought it was cool the way they shared and showed their uniqueness.

Right then, he felt a twinge in his gut.

It occurred to him that when he was their age, he pretty much conformed. Okay, he really conformed. He didn't show people that there was anything unique about him. He blended in, on purpose. He remembered making so many "ordinary" choices during middle school, choices to avoid being noticed, to avoid being loud or wearing anything close to "uniquely him" clothing. He didn't say or do anything out of the norm, he avoided standing out... on purpose. Not only did he not want to 'look bad,' he didn't feel okay to be himself, and he really didn't know who he was. He didn't realize it then, but it struck him now, like a splash of cold water on his face. Back then, he was just trying to survive.

A wave of sadness swept over him. It radiated over his entire body like a warm, wet, heavy blanket... even his toes felt it. His heart began to hurt, much like he had experienced before. It was a deep ache, right in the middle of his chest. It felt like his heart was getting larger, breaking from the inside out, breaking free from the bondage of past constraints, of old misery.

Brian was oddly relieved, yet at the same time, he felt a deep profound sadness. It was as if he had become a warm, wet towel and he was being wrung out. The good news was that he knew the "old" was leaving him and that would create space for the "new." He took a few breaths and started to move the feelings through him. With each breath, with each exhale, another wave of fears made their way out of him.

He went inside and found a quiet space against a wall in a side hallway. He leaned into it and took a few more breaths. More tears welled up from inside him. He let some flow through him and down his face. A subtle weight lifted as his heart opened up, it felt warm, like it was glowing. He gently wiped away his tears so no one would notice.

Who needs movies when I have experiences like this? he laughed.

After a few minutes, and some more deep breaths, he walked out of the hallway. On one level, Brian felt exhausted, worn out. On another, he felt renewed, like he'd been hollowed out. It was as if fresh, clean water was now coursing through his body - water with a power he hadn't recognized in years. He recognized it and greeted it, like a long lost friend.

It occurred to him that this "power" had been masked by his life, by the decisions and conclusions he had made over the years.

Brian found his way across the gym, which was now in full use. A dozen or so kids were shooting hoops and messing around. Brian had shifted. He was beaming, aglow with life.

He headed over to the homework room expecting chaos, after all, that was how he remembered it. He braced himself as he walked up to the doorway. He walked in and found eight or so young people seated at tables, you guessed it, actually doing homework. A smile crossed his face as he saw Tammie helping them with questions from their day. There was another young man, a tall one, helping as well. He looked like a college type.

He walked over to Tammie, said "Hi" again, and asked if he could help.

"Sure," she said. "What's your bailiwick?"

"Bailiwick? What's a bailiwick?" he chuckled.

"It's your area of expertise, silly."

"Ah, okay. Well, that would be Computer Science splashed in with a bit of Algebra, Trig and Statistics... although the last ones you may want to kick the tires on first," he said with a grin.

"Okay, nice." She introduced him to the kids. "Guys and gals, this is Brian. He can lend a hand if you'd like. He's good with Computer Science, Algebra, Trigonometry and Statistics."

Three hands shot up.

Brian walked over to the back right corner of the room and introduced himself to a young lady named Tabitha.

"I'm having a heck of a time with my algebra homework," she said. "Okay, algebra period. I honestly don't care what 'C' is. We solve for this and for that, without numbers and it's, well, freaky hard."

"I see," Brian said. "Let me take a look." As he looked at her paper his old math skills flooded back in. He loved algebra and was proud of the 4.0 he'd gotten in college, mainly because he hated it when he was in junior high. It looked like he and Tabitha had some common ground.

"Here's the deal," he said as he squatted down to get to her eye level. "It's like a rhythm or dance. Once you get the moves, it's easy peasy."

Where did "Easy Peasy" come from?

"Easy peasy? Easy peasy?" Tabitha asked.

Brian smiled and laughed. "Yeah, you know… simple."

"Ahhhhhh. Okaaaaay," she said in a doubtful and "Where'd YOU come from?" voice.

"You see, what you do on the right side you do on the left." Brian showed her some of the overarching techniques he'd learned. "Also, have you noticed that at about forty-five to fifty minutes in, your eyes roll back, like your brain is full?"

"Yes, Yes!!! That's what happens. He keeps on talking and all I hear are 'Wah, wah' sounds, and his lips keep on moving."

Brian laughed. "You might consider letting him know that, in a sweet way. My algebra teacher knew about it and she would look at the class around that time to check. She had a great way of letting us 'digest' things. She told us she knew that's what happens and since algebra builds each day, you need to digest it so you get the next step. If not, it makes things, well, freaky hard."

"Got it. I'll do that," she paused. "Um, he's mean though."

"What do you mean?"

"Well, my teacher is big and gruff and if you don't get things, he gets kind of mad."

"Humm... Have you talked to your folks about this?"

"My mom. She's busy and doesn't get algebra at all."

"Ok. Let's see. Well, you might try talking with your mom first and then him. That way, she has your back if you need, okay?"

"Okay. What about Mr. Gruff, though?"

"Well, what happens inside when you think about talking to him?"

She paused for a second, then said, "I get kind of queasy inside, and fluttery - not in a good way. Then I get afraid."

"Are you willing to try something?"

She scrunched her face and said, "Sure."

"When you walk up to him to talk, take a deep breath. Only let your brain focus on what you're going to talk about. No 'this will happen' or 'that will happen.' No, 'what if's,' okay?"

"Okay."

"Then, just be honest with him. See what he says and then look at the results to see what the next step is."

"Got it."

"Good. One more thing."

"Yes."

"Does he have times where you can go to him with questions?"

"Not really. We have a pretty tight schedule and like ten minutes between classes. I have a home room at fourth period, though."

"Well, you might see if he's available during that time. It's okay to ask for help, Tabitha. You're important and asking, well, that's up to you – to ask for things *because* you're important, see? Not better than others, just, as important as they are."

"Hey, are you some algebra, trig counselor or something?"

Brian laughed again. "Not really, not officially anyway," he laughed some more.

One seed planted.

After helping Tabitha, he helped a few more kids and went out and shot hoops with some others. At the end of the day, he noticed he was feeling nervous around Tammie. He felt like a high schooler again. He wondered if this was a good thing, or not.

3

A week went by and he'd spent several days working at the club. Things were going well. It was new, yet something was off for him.

He woke up that Wednesday morning and he felt right as rain. He got his morning run in and went back to his favorite diner for breakfast. He secretly was hoping to see the old man again.

Nothing. Nada. Zip. Bubkis.

He felt a bit bummed. His heart was a bit low as he got out of his booth to leave. On his way to the door he remembered the connection he had with the old man. He felt a wave of compassion, strength and support. It was if his past had become present and the old man was with him, right now.   He pulled open the door and the bell rang. A smile crossed his face.

The warm friendly sound of a diner door. Nice!

Feeling better, he hopped into his Range Rover and headed to the club for work. Something started to not feel right again. He couldn't quite put his finger on it, it was as if something was going to happen.

As he pulled into the parking lot he saw William talking with Tammie. They were having a rather heated argument, and well, it didn't look like it was going well for her. William saw him and both he and Tammie went into the building.

Brian parked, took a deep breath and headed inside.

This must have been what was off.

Brian went into the main office and clocked in. The conversation between Tammie and William was over and they were both sitting at their desks. The tension in the room was palpable, like a thick, humid day with a crispy edge to it. Brian felt the tension in his body.

Brian broke the silence. "Hi," he said.

"Hello," they both said in a subdued tone.

Okay, Brian thought. *Let's see how this unfolds.*

He glanced up at the clock and saw that he still had a few minutes before the "sea of kids" started.

"I'll go and get the homework room set up," Brian remarked.

"Sounds good," they said.

He walked over to the homework room and a grin showed up on his face. He flicked on the lights and straightened up here and there. Tammie walked in, she looked a bit shaken up.

"You okay?" he asked.

"Yeah, I'm good," she said. Brian could tell she was lying.

"Well, if you need, I have a great pair of ears," he said with a smile.

She sniffled and rubbed the tears away from her left cheek. "Thanks. Maybe later, okay?"

The kids poured in and Tammie and Brian went about their business. Tabitha showed up. He hadn't seen her since last they talked, and he was curious to see how things went.

"How'd it go?" he asked.

"Great," she said, then a frustrated look appeared on her face. "Well…mostly great."

Brian got down to her eye level. "I told my mom," she continued. "She was okay with me talking to the guy. The guy though, man. What a bummer."

"What do you mean?"

"Well, I used the trick you taught me. When I walked up to him, it worked great. I asked for what I wanted, explained what was going on for me and asked for help. It didn't work though. Mr. Gruff said, she deepened her voice in a fakey tone, "'It's your responsibility to keep up with the work, not mine.' He did say he could help me a couple of times a week, though.

He has thirty minutes twice a week during my homeroom. He was a jerk," she added, frowning.

"That's good news," blurted Brian.

"Didn't you hear what I said? He was mean, he hasn't changed and I'm still behind!"

"I did. Did *you* hear what you said?" he laughed.

"Oh, geez. I feel a lesson coming on here, mister. Go ahead," she said with a fake look of chagrin.

"Brace yourself," he laughed. "First, you asked for what you wanted, awesome, and second, you advocated for yourself. You said you're having challenges, which is great by the way…" he paused. "Um, not the challenge part…" he smiled. "And, 'C', you got some of what you wanted. Atta way!"

"Hey, what?! What a minute. First, you went one, two, 'C', what's up with that? And, second, didn't you hear? He was a jerk! He said it was my problem, not his."

"Ah, well, the one, two, 'C' was just me being weird… I put the 'L' in weird," Brian laughed. "About the teacher, well, he may have said that, yet, what were his actions? What did he really say?"

"What do you mean?" she asked.

"Wait for iiiiiit!" Brian said with an encouraging smile.

Tabitha took a deep breath. Brian realized how much he appreciated her patience and the way she learned… how she understood things, how she listened.

"Well," she said. "He's not helping me a lot, but he is helping."

"Exactly. Here's the deal. If you get caught up in the way someone says something, or if they're cranky, you can miss some things. Plus, what they say and do, well, that's just information. YOU get to decide what to do based on what they do, see?"

"Actuuuualllly… um, no."

"How about I drop a bit of history knowledge on you?"

"Gooo ahead," she said with a feigned reluctance and an exaggerated eye roll.

"Do you know who John F. Kennedy was?"

"Yea, sure. He was that president that got shot."

"Right. Well, while he was president there was a major incident that presented itself to him, it was called The Cuban Missile Crisis. You see, Russia put some nuclear missiles in Cuba, just off the coast of Florida."

"Okaay," she said, seriously wondering where this was going.

"Well, Kennedy put a blockade of ships up to prevent Russia from doing more in Cuba. Russia's guy, Khrushchev, got cranky about it and threatened to storm through the blockade. He even said the 'blockade' was an act of war."

"Dang! Yeah, I remember now. Not fun!"

"Right. Well, here's the deal. Khrushchev sent Kennedy quite a few letters. They were pretty negative, antagonistic and adversarial."

"Adversarial?"

"Yea, like fighting, wanting to go to war…not on the same page."

"Ah."

"Well, in late October, Kennedy got a letter from Khrushchev and it sounded much, much different. The language and tone were actually reasonable. Khrushchev said he'd pull out of Cuba if the U.S. agreed not to invade."

"Okaaaay," she said.

"Well, the very next day, Kennedy got another letter from him. It sounded the same as the others, cranky and mad, see?"

"Um, no."

"Well, Kennedy figured all the cranky letters were sent because of the political pressure that Khrushchev was going through.

"But wait, there's more! Here's the part that took some enormous courage. Kennedy decided to believe that the nice letter was what

Khrushchev really meant and he ignored the last mean, cranky letter. He decided to act and believe as though Khrushchev meant well and didn't actually want war. It was like the other letters weren't him, it was someone else. See?"

"Hang on a second. Wait... I heard what you said, but I think you're wanting me to find a deeper meaning that I can use." She paused for a few seconds.

Click.

"Got it! You're saying, go on what you want to hear or what you think the truth is. Sometimes people wear, like, costumes and don't mean what they say," she paused again. "Wait, wait for it!" A few seconds passed. "Ah, and sometimes people may even mean what they say, but they don't know that they don't. I get it! I get it!"

"Bingo," he paused. "Sometimes they're 'unconscious' and don't even know they do it. So, bring it back to Mr. Gruff. You said he was a bit cranky and that it was your responsibility, right?"

"Yes. Um hum."

"Well, is there truth in that? Lose the way he said it."

"Okay," she hesitated. "Well yes, to a point. He could teach better."

"Did you see Star Wars Episode 4?" Brian asked.

"Yes, I love Star Wars."

"Do you remember when they were attacking the Death Star, one of the pilots said," Brian mimicked the actor's voice... "Stay on target. STAAAAAY on taaargeet!"

"Yea, yea, I remember."

"Well, Tabitha... you didn't stay on target."

"Wha?" she paused then laughed. "Oh, yea, I see. Okay. So, you're saying: Don't get caught up in what I think about him personally or blame him."

"Bing - go! You see, if you get too caught up in the anger, it'll keep you from moving forward, from asking and getting what you want. Anger is okay. It's not about avoiding it, it's about mastering it and knowing what serves you best, see?"

"Okay, so, I'm having a hard time and he's willing to help. Now what?"

"Now, keep asking. Show up to those times. Do your best not to let your frustration get the better of you and…"

"Yes?"

"Study your butt off," he laughed.

"Waaaaiiiit. This doesn't sound easy."

"You only eat an elephant one bite at a time."

"You are weird."

"I know," he laughed. "Also, I'll be around. If not, you can ask Hank, the tall guy. He's good with Algebra, too. Have some patience, Tabitha. You're smart. You'll get it. Believe in yourself, do your best and let go of the outcome. Remember who you are and don't let anyone, not even your brain, tell you, or convince you, otherwise."

"What?"

Where was this stuff coming from?

"Just do your best and don't worry about what happens. Doing your best and believing in yourself, that's all that's important. Deal?"

"Deal!"

He wondered where he got all this knowledge from. He realized it was great information and that he ought to heed it, too!

The next day he woke up and felt off again. There was no other way to explain it, he just didn't feel right. He got into his running gear, hopped into his rig and went to his favorite running spot. He had a great run - he was blank, in the zone and not thinking. He finished, tired, sweaty… and he felt great. He stopped for a minute, took in the fresh air and the gorgeous view of the city. Suddenly, things clicked for him, like a gear softly falling into place in a car. Once it clicks, there's a connection - it engages and you can move.

The thing nagging at him was:

"I'm not looking forward to going to work."

He liked the time he spent with the kids, but it felt like "work" to him.

That's it.

The Boy's and Girl's Club had become work.

I don't want to work for a living. I want to do what I love and have the living… the money, follow.

That's a good one! he laughed. *I need to write that down somewhere.*

He walked back to his rig, toweled off and found a 3 x 5 card in his glove box. In bold black lettering he wrote down the phrase:

> I am doing what I love for a living.

He wedged it in a seam of the plastic on his dash.

That'll help, he thought. *I'll be able to keep my mind focused that way.*

He ran a few errands, went back to his place and read a bit until it was time to go to work. As he was sitting there, he reflected on his last year. He'd been through so much. He felt some pride well up from within him. A year ago, when problems would happen he would reach for his dad's silver flask and take a pull of bourbon. Now, when something is going on, he goes for a run or does one of his "walks of blankness." He doesn't try to "figure" out things near as much these days and he waits until the answers come – he waits for things to show up.

Who would have thought?

Exactly.

Brian chuckled out loud. He remembered the fact that William, from the Boys and Girls club, called him out of the blue. That wouldn't have happened if he hadn't checked into teaching, and that wouldn't have happened if he hadn't left Micro Tech. He laughed and remembered a phrase he had read from Goethe or Murray, he wasn't sure who.

The gist was:

> *Until one is committed there is hesitancy, the chance to draw back...*

Whatever you can do, or dream you can, begin it.

Boldness has genius, power, and magic in it…

At the moment one definitely commits oneself, then Providence moves, too.

A smile formed on his face and he wondered how Tammie was doing. Just then, the phone rang. It was the club, he swiped right. "Hi, this is Brian."

"Hi Brian, it's Tammie. Say, would you be up for meeting for lunch before work today?"

Ugh, there's that word again. "Work."

"Sure, I'd be glad to. Where and when?"

"How about Marko's Café in an hour?"

"Deal. See you there, then."

He was tickled inside. His heart flipped and it was accompanied by a bit of a flutter. He liked her. He liked her quite a bit.

He got to Marko's a few minutes early and looked at the card on his dash. It occurred to him that something was missing from it, it wasn't quite complete. He'd check that out after the lunch date. Well, wait. Was it a date?

Don't be attached to things.

Show up and see what happens.

Let your life unfold - don't force your life.

If you force things, it changes the layout.

He walked into the café and found a cute booth by the window. He liked booths. Tammie arrived shortly after him, dressed for work. She walked in and their eyes met. She looked gorgeous. Oh, and yes, his heart flipped in his chest again.

He stood up as she came to the booth.

"Hi," she said with a wide smile.

"Hi," Brian said.

He wanted to say, "You look great," but he didn't know, yet, if it was a date or not.

"Thanks," she said with a twinkle and a smile.

They both sat down, opposite from each other.

"What's up?"

"Nothing really, I just wanted to get to know you better," she said, "and ask your advice. You seem so great with the kids."

"Sure," Brian said. He was sweating a bit. That was interesting.

"Advice, or 'get to know me better,' first?" he asked.

"Get to know you better," she laughed. "Where are you from? I know William said you're new to the area and all."

"I'm from Seattle, Redmond actually. Born in L.A., raised there."

"Have you been married?"

"Once. It didn't work out."

"I'm sorry."

"No, it's okay. It wasn't meant to be and something good will come from it." Brian smiled. He realized he had come a long way.

"What's that mean?"

"Well, I learned a lot from it, and I'm much more clear about who I want to be with," he said with a smile. "It made space for the right woman, you know? How about you?"

"No, never married. I was born in Boston, I came over here seven years ago. I have a degree in biology from Arizona State University. Go Devils!" she laughed.

"Biology, huh. How does that connect to the working at the club thing?"

She giggled, "It doesn't, really. I just kind of fell into it."

"Biology or the club?" he asked with a grin.

"Both," she smiled and laughed.

"Nice," he paused. "Hey, so I noticed you and William got into a bit of an argument yesterday. Do you mind if I ask what happened?"

"No, that's okay. I wanted more hours and a promotion to regional and he was being stubborn. He won't give me a good reference because he wants me to stay here. I'm pretty bummed, really, and a bit torqued off too, now that you mention it."

"It looked like he said some mean things."

"Yeah, yeah he did. He reminded me of my father actually. Let's just say, what he said wasn't very supportive of who I am. I've decided I'm going to leave, Brian. It's not working out for me and, well, he doesn't treat me very well."

"I understand. Good for you for noticing."

"You don't get caught up in drama much, how come?"

"It's overrated," he chuckled. "Besides, something good usually comes out of things like this. It's not that what he did was okay, to me it's more like your life is telling you something." Brian had this sudden feeling like he went too far with her.

He remembered the old man saying, "Gather the information, Brian. Ask direct questions."

"Did I step over the line with you with my last question?"

"You mean the something good part, or the life is telling you part?" she asked.

"Both."

She laughed. "Nope, you're good. It's pretty smart actually, it makes sense. I knew you were a good egg."

They both smiled. From there it was a typical lunch date and he was glad that's what it was. He was curious what their relationship was supposed to be.

Don't force things. Show up, don't be attached to the outcomes.

See what things are supposed to be. Life just works out better that way.

Whoever said that, wherever it came from, was right on.

They paid for their lunch and she gave him a sweet hug as they left the café.

"See you in a few," she said.

"Looking forward to it," he said with a grin.

Interesting. Life is so interesting.

Brian was excited for what was coming.

He headed into work. As he pulled into the parking lot, he looked at his card on the dash and it struck him, again. The missing piece. He loved hanging out with and helping the kids, he also liked spending time with Tammie... it felt like work to him, though. He knew there wasn't such a thing as a "perfect" livelihood. There'll always be something you do in a career that you don't like, for him, there were quite a few things that were off here. He knew it in his bones.

That afternoon and evening, his work went off without a hitch. William let him know that Tammie had given notice and asked if he was interested in the position.

"No, thank you," Brian said. "I appreciate you thinking of me, though."

"No sweat, William," he said. Brian knew he wasn't long for here, either. He'd miss the kids, but it just didn't feel right.

The next morning, before his morning run, he asked himself the question:

What do I love to do... where I lose all sense of time?

Rather than answer it, he just held the question in his awareness as he ran. His run went great, he felt refreshed, relaxed and at peace. He had breakfast and noticed he still hadn't gotten an answer.

Interesting, he thought.

Maybe not today, but I know it's coming.

He knew that he'd be giving notice soon. As a courtesy, he'd find out how William was doing with staffing first. He didn't want to leave him in a lurch, and it wasn't a hurry for him, either.

He showed up for work a bit early, knowing things were coming to a close. He felt clear about it and oddly excited, not so much about leaving, it was more about being excited about what was coming.

He started walking into Williams' office just as Tammie was coming out. She had tears in her eyes.

"Are you okay?" Brian asked.

"Yeah, I'm good," she said as she wiped away the tears.

"Are you sure?"

"Yeah, yeah. I'm okay," she sniffled.

"Are you up for dinner tonight?" Brian asked.

"Sure," she said.

"Where?"

"How about Pietro's? They've got great Italian."

"Sure. Seven?"

"Deal, see you there," and she headed to the front doors to leave.

Brian was giddy. A part of him had woken up, a part of him that had been asleep for a long, long time. Plus, he liked how easy it was with her. Within two heart beats, fear started flooding in – it engulfed him and he started to sweat. His brain started coming up with "What if's" out the wazzu. "What if the problem with William is a sign? Maybe she's had a torrid past and this thing won't work. You're not good enough for her anyway." He was in a flat spin again.

Wow and Stop!

He paused for a second, took a deep breath and was able to watch his thoughts. An image appeared of him as a little boy, about nine or ten, trying to figure everything out. He was in his room, standing on his bed with his hands on his hips. He was wearing an adorable white with red trim t-shirt. On the front were words: Super Protector.

Brian's here and now body tightened up. He focused on the image again. It appeared as though little Brian thought he had a job to do, and he was taking it very seriously. He was thinking so hard, his little brow was furrowed.

He took a deep breath. "This, I have to go over with the old man."

That night, another dream started. This time, Brian was in a bright yellow sports car, a 2017 Ford GT to be exact – a gorgeous piece of machinery. It was nighttime, around 11:30 p.m. and he was heading down a windy, desert road at a moderate pace for the car. The twin turbo V-6 motor hummed as it pumped well over 600 horsepower to its rear wheels.

The asphalt was pitch black, dotted only by the blurred yellow lines whisking by him on the left and the clear white arching illumination of the gorgeous machine's LED headlights.

Outside, it was still over 90 degrees and there was no one to be seen. No traffic, no towns, nothing- just the occasional tall standing cactus whisking by the side of the road.

Brain was exhilarated. He felt the firmness of the steering wheel, the hum of the motor, the grip of the car… but he was flat out lost.

You see, the car's GPS wasn't working, he didn't have a phone and there were no road signs. None. Zip. Nada. He was in third gear and was going way too fast, the speedometer read 128. A quick left turn showed up in front of him and he was too late to hit the apex. As a matter of fact, his driving line was way off… he was going to miss the corner completely.

He yanked the steering wheel hard to the left. The front tires obeyed but the back end of the car flew out from under him, stubbornly continuing to the right. He might as well have been on ice.

The car careened from the pitch black asphalt onto the red dirt shoulder, it's tires spewing red dust everywhere. The back end momentum twisted the car sideways and the dirt and gravel screamed as it tried to grip the tires. Brian had lost control.

He felt a moment of hope as he felt the car come back under him, just for a millisecond, then his hope was abruptly snuffed out. The car was no longer his.

With his heart pounding in his ears and chest, the car flung him off the road, off the earth and over the side of the mountain. Brain was now in the center of a slow, powerful, sideways rotation. His seatbelt was keeping him pinned into his leather seat.

The bottom dropped out suddenly. With his stomach in his throat, Brian was now tumbling towards the red rocks quietly waiting for him below. The centrifugal force was immense. He was being flung forward into the stiff fabric seatbelt, then smashed sideways into the beige and black door panel, up into the headliner and then thrown back into his leather seat. He was being buffeted around like a rag doll in a dryer.

As he and the car were plummeting towards the waiting rocks, Brian caught glimpses of the sky and stars, the moonlit cliff and then the ravine, over and over and over again. He was on his way to his death and he knew it. Soon, he would be compressed into the car's interior as it smashed onto the red rocks below, well over five hundred feet from where he started.

He started to scream as the word "Stop!" formed in his voice.

He lurched forward in bed, screaming as he opened his eyes.

"Holy …." he shouted through his sweat soaked t-shirt. He was breathing heavily and his body still felt like it was tumbling downward to the earth.

He looked around and got his bearings.

"Everything is okay," he said softly to himself. "Everything is okay."

He slowly got out of bed, flicked on the light and went into the kitchen. He was still sweating as he grabbed a glass from the counter, opened the fridge and poured himself some ice cold water. He backed the glass and realized his heart was pounding.

What the…? That was so real… and I wasn't even there…

He took some deep breaths, gathered himself and went out to his balcony to settle down.

Tears formed from inside him and worked their way out of his body. He was being wrung out again.

He was shaking.

Inhale. Exhale. Inhale. Exhale. The tears continued to flow and after a few moments, he was able to think clearly again.

Okay, Brian. Okay. I got this. This is nothing new. Life is trying to tell me something. It'll come. It will come.

He took a deep breath and headed back to bed.

Old man, I could really use a sit down with you right now.

Instantly, he heard the familiar sound of the old man whistling that song, the one he could almost place. He knew he'd be ok.

After a bit, he calmed down, picked up a Star Wars book and read himself to sleep.

4

He ended up at his favorite diner that morning, his run done and his appetite big. He went to his normal booth, by the window thank you, and ordered his favorite omelet and orange juice. The emotions from his dream were right on the surface - it wouldn't take much for them to spill over again. Just then, the bell rang above the door.

An instant feeling of relief washed over him.

A smile emerged on his face as he saw the old man in the fedora walk into the diner. The old man smiled, winked at the waitress and headed over to him, whistling that familiar song. Right now, it didn't even matter what the song was, Brian was flat out glad to see him. He had so many questions.

The old man slid into the booth, "Hiya kiddo."

Brian couldn't figure out how he did it. The old man looked so young, so happy, so alive. Amazing.

"Hi old man. Am I glad to see you!"

"I'll bet," he paused, "What's up?"

"Plennn ty!" chimed Brian. "I have so many questions, really."

"Well, what's important?"

"The car dream from last night. It really messed me up."

"Go on..."

Brian explained how real the dream felt, how he literally felt like he was falling to his death.

"I see," the old man said.

"My life, it's like driving a new car," Brian continued. "A high end sports car. It does…. I'm doing… all these new things I never thought, or knew, a 'car' could do."

"You're right on, Brian. You're open, Brian… more self-aware. It's not a bad thing. There are things happening that either weren't possible before, when you were you're old self, or they happened and you didn't notice, or your brain wouldn't let you notice." The old man chuckled.

"Don't worry about figuring it all out right now, Kiddo. You'll get it if you're supposed to."

"I have so many questions, though."

"Go ahead," the old man smiled.

"Well, wait a second." It occurred to him that all of the questions he had, ones he'd write down or tell himself to remember either faded away with time or were answered. He was beginning to think that they weren't as important as he thought.

"No, I'm good Old Man, I'm good. It's good to see you."

"You too, Kiddo. Well…"

"You're on a schedule," Brian interrupted with a smile.

"Yes. Yes I am," he added with a smile and a twinkle in his eye.

Brian felt like he needed a bit of down time, some solace to digest his meeting with the old man and flat out, a break from it all. He headed up to Camelback Mountain, parked at the base and went for a walk. As the sun beat down on him, he immediately started to feel better. He noticed the warmth of the crunchy red earth beneath his feet; the air, its warmth surrounding him like a friendly blanket. He looked up and noticed a bird circling him in the sky. Tears welled up. He took a deep breath, taking in all he had accomplished. He realized how proud he was of himself, truly proud of himself.

He took another step and felt a wave of gratitude grow from within him. It started at the base of his spine and sent a positive wave of energy through his body. It was thick, warm and immensely joyful and loving. It came in waves, much like the ribbon candy that comes at Christmas time, only not quite as sweet.

This feeling enveloped his whole body, truly, he was feeling love and joy… the depth and breadth of it were immense. He felt like he was connected to everything around him, the rocks, the earth, the sky…the air. He felt so comfortable, so complete, so at ease – at peace from the inside out. This was an unusually foreign and entirely welcome feeling. He felt a presence, like he was loved and not alone. As he glanced around at the red rocks, the palpable feeling he was experiencing reached beyond him and seemed to reach outward for several hundred feet. It was as if the warmth, the fabric he was experiencing, was telling him he was not alone.

In that moment, he knew, from the core of his being, that he was really on the right track. He got how wonderful his life was, how fortunate he was to recognize it and to be on this path. He knew that and that all would be okay, actually, more than okay. He was a partner in his own life now and there was something else with him, guiding him. He remembered the conversation he had with Peter:

> "Once I realized there was something else on my side, I let up quite a bit.…I stopped chasing all those 'micro fears' that showed up each day. Once I eased up, my life improved dramatically… things happened in ways I could never have planned."

No longer was Brian "figuring" it out, reacting from past experiences or creating the life he thought he was "supposed" to be living. He got that now he was truly free.

It had been quite the week for Brian, quite the month, really. He had a new dream telling him something, he wasn't sure about Tammie, he was getting ready to quit his new job and was tempted to call Melinda - even though he knew it was over with her.

The good news was that he knew what he "didn't" want to do. He knew he wanted to do something with kids, yet the whole school thing didn't fit, neither did the Boys and Girls Club.

After his morning run, shower and shave, he decided to hit the nearby diner, secretly hoping to see the old man. He truly felt grateful for knowing him.

His meal was wonderful, yet no old man.

Later that week, he'd gone to work a bit early and gave his two weeks' notice to William, who had received it well. William appreciated that Brian wasn't leaving him in a lurch.

Midway through, William brought in a new hire, Miya. She was in her thirties and she had been a teacher for a few years. Apparently she wanted to create something larger, to reach children on a broader and deeper scale. She had gotten a degree in psychology and wanted to work with children, to support them to lead happier, safer, more fulfilling lives.

He introduced himself, she smiled and they started the "small talk." She was very cordial. Apparently, her parents were from Seattle, too.

"Interesting," Brian said.

"Yes, isn't it?" she laughed.

It's funny how our lives intertwine with others, he thought.

"Where did you go to school?" he asked.

"I went to Cleveland High School. I ..." He heard her say something else, then the words "Math team, debate and chess club." He wasn't sure why he had stopped listening. He checked in and noticed he felt like he was glowing.

"What the...? Breathe.

He was instantly whisked to the diner...

He heard the old man say, "Trust. Stay present. Be yourself. Unfold your life. Hold it, don't force it. Like a butterfly, you can crush it if you push."

Brian was whisked back to the here and now.

Brian focused back on the moment.

He picked up where he left off.

"Daaaang, remind me not to play chess with you. Math, huh? What was the draw for you?"

"Well, I always liked the way things flowed in math, plus the sense of completion, really. That and that numbers never lie."

"Nice," Brian said. They talked more, got to know each other and he realized he really liked her. She was sweet and seemed like she would be great with the kids.

Miya and Brian greeted the "sea of kids," and headed into the homework room. The kids in the homework room liked her, too.

That Saturday, he slept in a bit and took a day off from his running routine. He didn't, however, let go of heading to his favorite diner for breakfast.

The door creaked as he walked in and the familiar jingle from the bell above the door brought a smile to his face. He took a long whiff of the freshly brewed coffee and spotted his favorite booth in the corner. For grins, he decided to grab an orange soda on his way back.

He landed, took a pull from his drink and decided to try something new. Pancakes with two eggs over easy and sausage, thank you. The waitress came over, took his order with a smile and headed off. The bell above the door jingled - it was the old man in a new fedora. He was smiling from ear to ear and whistling the same old tune. It no longer bothered Brian that he couldn't place it.

His heart leapt as the old man winked at him, gave the waitress a smile and sat down across from him. He let out a playful sigh as he slid into the booth.

"How are you doing, Son?"

Son? He's never called me that before.

"Been better, been worse, how about you?"

"Any day you get up to is a good one. Are you a Yankees fan?"

"No, you?"

He began to wonder where the conversation was going. Usually, the old man was pretty direct in his, well, indirectness. This time, it was like he was working his way in from the outside, the far, far outside.

"Not so much, not since the days of Gehrig, Mantle and DiMaggio," the old man smiled. "Did you ever play?" he asked.

"I played in a high school... couldn't hit the curve, so I stopped."

"How many times did you strike out?"

"Tons I guess. Why?"

"Humor me. How many times did you go to bat?"

"I dunno," Brian actually found himself getting frustrated. "What's the point?"

"Work with me here," he laughed. "Here's the deal. An average baseball player these days gets on base only twenty-six percent of the time. Twenty six percent," he chuckled. "It's been pretty much that way for quite a while, even during the steroid era," he laughed.

"Anyway, let's say a batter gets 200 official at bats in a season…"

"Old man, I like you, really I do. What's the point here?"

The old man still had a grin on his face, "Patience, Brian. Patience. The story sometimes is better than the point," he winked. "Where was I? Ah. So, the ball player gets 200 official at bats and if he's average, he gets on base fifty-two times," he laughed. "Fifty-two times out of 200. Do you see, Brian?" The old man was still grinning.

"No, Old Man, I don't." Brian almost choked on the words. He knew he was getting mad and his anger was getting the better of him. He took a deep breath.

"Wait a minute. I think I get it," Brian said.

He really didn't.

Patience. Breathe…

"What on earth does this have to do with the fact that I don't have a job, that I don't know what I'm doing with my life or if I want to stay with my wife? Don't you get it?"

Brian realized that he was way off kilter. His anger was running him - it was driving his choices.

The old man sat across from him, quiet and patiently smiling. Waiting.

Breathe.

"Okay," Brian let out his long breath. "I think what you're saying is that it would be easy to look at things, at life, in a negative way." He paused for a second, then continued, "I'm also getting that when you focus on the negative, you give up. It would be easy for your brain to make things worse than they are, to lose perspective.

"So, a major league ball player might think he isn't good enough when he thinks of all the times he doesn't get on base. They have to believe in themselves. They focus on the times, the things that worked, on what got them there.

"Ok. Okay, I see...In order to be a success, even in hitting .300, it takes faith."

The old man laughed out loud, "That's it exactly!!!" he exclaimed. "You ARE a quick study!

"It also takes patience, Brian. Patience and trust. There are so many strategies to hitting. My favorite is to know what you're looking for and wait for that pitch. Sometimes it comes early in the at bat, usually not, though. Did you know that quite a few hitters take the first pitch?"

"Yeah, so?"

"Well, it takes patience, trusting in themselves and in the process, even if it's a strike, see? They know the count, how many chances they have and they believe in themselves."

Breathe.

The old man went on. "You see, when it gets in their head that they're 'failing,' they start focusing on that and forget to do the things that had worked for them before. Ballers call it 'pressing.' When they press, they can play themselves out of baseball. Actually, they don't 'play' themselves out, they 'brain' themselves out," he laughed. "It's a mental game, my friend, and a game of perspective and patience."

Brian felt like he was drinking from a full on three inch fire hose pumping at 200 p.s.i.. He was drowning in information and needed a break.

"Can we stop for a minute?"

"Sure," the old man said.

They sat there for several minutes. Brian felt his energy leaving - he was getting so, so tired. His brain was trying so hard to "figure out" what was going on, it was actually making things harder. Much like algebra, he was stuck, trying to figure things out.

Click

I get it, Brian thought. *I'm so focusing on what's not working that I'm not moving forward in my life.*

Brian blurted, "I'm trying to figure out Tammie, Melinda and my career, instead of showing up and knowing."

"Bingo!" the old man said.

"I get it," Brian added. "Show up and quit trying to figure it out."

"Exactly."

Brian paused for a second. He realized he was feeling a bit vulnerable. "Old Man, I'm scared. These are uncharted waters for me. I'm not sure I'm up for it. It's a little unsettling and, well, I'm scared."

"You're up for it, Kiddo. You are... you just don't know it yet." He left a twenty on the table and headed out the door. "Until next time," he said as he swiped his right index finger across his new fedora. "Be well."

"But...."

This is nothing like the other meetings, he mused. *I wonder if it's the fear.*

It was. He knew it was.

Brain sat for a few minutes, gazing out the window. Blank hard drive, ROM off, computer not processing - no screen, no blinking cursor, nothing. Not thinking, thank you.

After about thirty minutes, Brian rebooted. He remembered he had a dinner date with Tammie. He paid for his food, hopped in his rig and headed over to meet her. He still, mostly, was not thinking.

He found her at a table just inside the door. As he sat down, he realized how much he really liked her. He was scared about things when he thought of the future, yet he really liked her. He also knew, deep down, that things with Melinda were over - he was done.

It was so easy to be with Tammie.

"I'm going into med school," she said.

"Nice... wait a minute. Where?" He felt the fear come up and he was disgusted with himself.

"Well, I've applied to The University of Arizona and I'm hoping to start in the fall."

"Awesome," he said - amidst a mixture of his stomach flipping, turning sour and his heart being happy.

Breathe. Everything happens for a reason.

"How will the Sun Devils feel," he chuckled. He wasn't sure what to do with all this information. In fact, his stomach was a jambalaya of emotions right now, a little bit of everything, all churning and brewing.

Breathe.

"They'll be okay," she smiled. "U of A" is the place for me, I checked it out and it's a great medical school. I hope all my Sun Devil buddies will be okay, though," she laughed. "It's only a couple hours away. What do you think?"

"I think it's great," Brian smiled. "Going for what you want is important. It's a bit unexpected, though." As the words came out of his mouth, he realized his fear was talking. He frowned inside.

Darn it.

The rest of the dinner went wonderfully. Brian was able to set aside his "future tripping," trying to figure out what, if anything, her change in plans meant. He was off though, he knew it. Several times, while sitting with her, Brian noticed his heart - it was warm from the inside out. He noticed how radiant, how beautiful she was. She even seemed to glow.

They ended their meal with some laughter. He walked her to her car, they embraced for a minute and kissed gently. Tammie let her hand linger in Brian's as he let go and headed to his car.

He woke up the next morning feeling alive, great to be inside his own skin. He was happy. He did his morning run and went to Brenda's, his favorite natural food store. He was 'jonesing' for a snack, some carbs and protein to be exact.

As he opened the door, he got a whiff of the place. Natural flour, fresh baked goods and the hint of scented candles. He liked this place. He liked places that were unique, that weren't "cookie cutter" and all sterile. This place had character, he liked that.

As he was heading back to the bakery section for a buttered croissant, he noticed the old man in a back aisle. He headed over and noticed he was grabbing a small bag of flour.

"Hi," the old man smiled.

"Hi," Brian said. "What's that for?"

"It keeps me young," the old man said as he winked at him. "It's an older flour, it doesn't have all that processing and additives. Amaranth," he smiled. "I like the taste. Hey, you wanna go for a walk when we're done here?"

"Sure," Brian said. "Thank you!"

Odd. He never asks me…

The old man bought his flour and some flax oil. Brain paid for a croissant he'd picked up and a couple of "Panda" natural licorices. He put the licorice in his pocket and took a bite of his croissant as they headed out for their walk.

"What's up?" the old man asked.

As they headed through the parking lot, Brian looked at his rig, the Range Rover. He realized that wasn't the car for him anymore.

"Well, to start, I know I don't want my rig anymore. I can feel it in my bones."

"Patience, Brian. Patience. It's one thing to know the truth, to know what's right for you. It's another to manifest it."

"Well played, Old Man. Well played. It's just that the emotions are so intense of late, it's a daily battle."

"Time takes time, Brian. Remember, your emotions are information, yet they're not emergencies. Think of all the times you've acted on your feelings, on impulse."

"Okay, I get it. I get it."

"What else is going on, really?" the old man asked.

"It's the dream I've been having, the one about the Ford GT. It's nagging at me, plus, still not knowing what I want to do is bugging me... and then there's Tammie. She's going to med school in Tucson and I have a feeling things are shifting. I was hopeful and now I'm bummed. I feel like I can't control things. Anything. I'm more than torqued off about this whole mess. I'm angry and I'm scared."

"What about that young lady, Miya, that showed up at work?"

"She's nice, nothing came of it, though."

"A wise man once told me: 'Phil, expectations are a setup for suffering.' You see, when we have them, it's like we're preparing a four course meal that we have to eat. When things don't work out, well, the meal is awful and every bite tastes bad."

"Okay, but once in a while I'd like things to go the way I want."

"Well, Kiddo, it has. Remember Micro Tech, Melinda and all that? Don't focus on what's not working, Brian. All it does is create fuel for the fear. Remember, your brain wants you to have problems, even when you don't, see?"

"I've been much happier since I realized that one," he laughed.

"Plus," he added. "You can't hear your own voice when you're in intense feelings and fear, Brian. You may 'hear' a voice, but it's the fear talking. Fear clouds and can take over your thoughts. Remember: Fear can't be trusted."

"It's like Yoda said: 'Fear leads to anger, anger leads to hate and hate leads to suffering.' He said it's the path to the dark side. I think it's more about keeping you from your sweet spot. You can't think of, or move towards what you want when you're in fear," he paused. "Get it?"

"Are you some old eccentric monk or something? Where do you get this stuff?"

"I'm just an average guy, like you, Brian. Just like you. Back to what we were talking about, okay?"

"Sure, Old Man, sure. I think I get it, it's just that, well… it's frustrating. It takes so dang long for it to move through."

The old man stopped for a minute, took a deep breath and looked around. He broke the silence. "Ahhhhh. What a beautiful day," he smiled as if he was trying to tell Brian something.

"Dang, Old Man. You're never direct, are you?" Brian laughed. "I get it… appreciate the day and stay in it. I get it."

"You bet, Kiddo. Any day you wake up to is a good one. Any day. All the other stuff is just stuff. It's your brain that wants to create happiness by controlling its environment, people, places and things. That's a setup to fail, you'll never be happy that way.

"Everything changes, Brian, that's the constant. Your brain sets you up to be miserable."

They stopped walking for several long, peaceful, seconds.

The old man continued, "I want you to know I heard all the other stuff you mentioned while we were walking. Have faith and believe in yourself. Things will unfold, Brian, if you let them. You'll know, Brian, you'll know. I heard you. Don't let your brain, don't let your fear get the better of you. You're a good man."

The old man smiled and said, "I need to head back, I have a schedule to keep," the old man winked.

Tears welled up from inside Brian, from deep, deep down. His heart ached a bit and he was warm. This may have been the first time anyone he cared about told him he was a good man.

"Deal, and thanks," Brian said. His heart sank into his stomach as he said the words and realized the old man was leaving. There was so much unresolved, so many questions he had.

They headed back to the store.

Funny, thought Brian. *When I don't fix things, I feel better. The air even smells sweeter now...*

They got back to the parking lot and with a wink and a tug of his fedora, the old man headed north on the highway.

Brian hopped in his rig and fired it up.

Who is that guy....really?

5

The next morning, Brian woke up feeling right as rain. He went for his run and sat with what he been told. He didn't think about anything, really, he more or less let things simmer. It occurred to him that the old man was right. He remembered the last time fear had shown up, how it immobilized him. How strong it was.

What if I fail?

I may never find a job I like.

The old man is nuts!

He rounded the corner by the familiar trees. He focused on the warmth of the air, how his breath and air filled his lungs. He noticed the cadence of his feet along with the rhythm of his breath. In, one, two, three, four... out, one, two, three, four. The plodding of his feet matched the rhythm of his breath. He glanced down at his feet, watching the blur as it blended in with his breath. He started to smile – he so loved his runs.

He let his arms drop and flop at his sides for a few strides, jiggling them a bit.

Midway through his run he realized his brain was putting up a fight and he fought back. He was so caught up fighting, struggling and listening to his fear that he didn't know where or when he was. His thinking was overrunning him, preventing him from being present to his life. He was frustrated and stopped.

This was harder than he thought. The more he thought about the fears, the bigger they became. It got to the point that he realized he couldn't control anything and it freaked him out a bit. He found himself second guessing his leaving the company, his not taking the CEO up on the job offer to be his aid and deciding to leave his wife. He was recycling the same fears. He was becoming afraid to be afraid.

It occurred to him to create a picture of a safe in his head, to visualize it and to tell his brain that he was putting his fear inside, and that he'd look at it later. The safe was huge, not a run of the mill home variety. It was a full on bank safe, complete with a two foot deep steel front and eighteen four inch tubes that ran from the edge of the door into the steel wall. It was a great safe.

He visualized himself putting all his fears inside and saw himself slamming the safe shut. The door closed and the steel posts moved into place with a resounding thud. He spun the spoked chrome wheel in front, sealing each of his fears inside.

A sense of relief flooded his body, the weight of the world had been lifted from him.

Awesome!

In, one, two, three, four… out, one, two, three, four. He ran for a few more minutes, taking in the day, the rhythm, the alive yet peaceful feeling he felt. Then, he realized he was thinking about getting a new car again. He realized he was having a full on conversation in his head for the last couple minutes. It wasn't prevalent, his main thought… the thinking was running in the back ground.

He laughed out loud. "Okay, my brain. I see you," he smiled. A few more breaths. "I got this," as he exhaled. "I got this." In, one, two, three, four. "Everything is okay." Inhale. "I'm not thinking about this now."

He put the fear back in his safe. He noticed just how sneaky his brain was. It would start to think about how to solve a problem, then the fear would leak in, like there was a back door open. The "solution" his brain would come up with always sounded innocuous enough, but he noticed that by listening to these thoughts, even by preparing to solve problems, it lead to the fear coming in the back door. It's like his thinking about a "problem" created a ripple in a pond that signaled it was okay to open the door and let the fear in.

He ended up back at his rig, feeling a bit frustrated about how tenacious his brain was. He reached for that old fedora he bought. He took a few moments, then put it on his head.

God, I hope no one is watching this…

He sat behind the wheel and took a deep breath.

What would the old man do?

He laughed, "He'd probably start whistling that stupid song."

"Hum humm.. We ain't got money, I'm so in love with you honey. Everything, will be all right…"

That was it!

Everything will be all right!

Brian 1. Brain 0

It was around 7:30 in the evening as he pulled up to the restaurant to meet Tammie for dinner. He walked in the door and saw her sitting on the bench nearby. His heart flipped, again, and he started to feel warm. They hugged, kissed briefly and the hostess guided them to a quiet seat in the back.

She had some more good news – it was official, she had been accepted to the med school and was super excited. He found himself jealous and scared at the same time.

"Very cool," Brian said. "I'm happy for you. You look so excited!"

"Thanks, Brian. I am."

"Can I ask you a question about it?"

"Sure."

"How did you know it was what you wanted to do?"

"Well, honestly, I don't. The truth is that I love medicine and seem to have a knack for it. I'm not sure it is exactly what I want to do, but if I don't try it, I'll never know, you know what I mean?"

Wow. She sounds just like the old man.

"How come you think this way?"

"I dunno. I was raised on a farm in Ohio and my dad was always super supportive. He also didn't make a big deal about failure or mistakes, he used to say, 'Pumkin', it's all about learning and growin', growin' and doin'.'"

"I'm super lucky. Most dads want their daughters to grow up and marry a lawyer or something. He wanted me to be happy. He was a great man. I still miss him." She started to tear up.

Brian felt his heart open and grow warm.

"I heard someone say that it's all about doing what you love, where you lose all track of time," he said. "I've noticed for me, it happens when I'm with kids, when I'm listening to them, and running. Okay, and baseball. Well, maybe I'll be a track and baseball coach for kids," he laughed.

"Whatever you love, Brian, do it."

Man I love her.

Whaat?

"Thanks, Tammie. You're sweet. I didn't mean to hijack the conversation, though. I think it's so cool you're going for it, going for what you want."

"Me, too," she said

"Tell me more," he added.

She shared more about the application process, her excitement about becoming a doctor and why she was so passionate about medicine. They talked, laughed and had a great dinner together. Brian really enjoyed his time with her. He walked her to her car, they hugged and she gave him a peck on the cheek.

"Night," Brian said.

"Night," she said. She got into her car and drove off. Brian called it an evening, and headed home. He slept well. No dreams.

Brian woke up refreshed, awake and relaxed. As he was getting his running gear, the impulse to call Tina showed up. He called her, said "Hi" and told her what he was up to.

"You know," she said, "a friend of mine's husband coaches at Middleton High School. Let me give her a call."

"That sounds great, Tina. Thank you."

"You bet," she said. "Glad to. I'll let you know what she says."

"Thanks, Tina." Brian swiped left, with a big grin on his face.

Patience, he thought. *The old man always talked about patience.*

He noticed and appreciated how many people were showing up, helping him. His heart warmed.

As he hung out at home, some thoughts started to form. He started to feel like a schmuck for not doing anything. All he was currently doing was showing up at a job with a week left on his notice, knowing he didn't want to work there and he didn't have a clue about what he wanted to do - according to his brain anyway.

Just then, the image of an old college friend of his named Peter popped into his head. He decided to call him. He pulled up his cell phone and called. He realized that that song the old man always whistled was playing in his head. He felt better already.

Brian heard a friendly, "Hello."

"Hi Peter, it's Brian from 'U Dub', remember me?"

"Hey. Yeah, Brian. How are you doing? Man, it's been forever. How are things?"

"Well, they're pretty good actually. A lots been going on for me the last few months."

"I heard. I saw on the news about the merger... they said you left the company. What was that about?"

"Basically, it wasn't a good fit for me. I was doing it for all the wrong reasons. Actually, that's partly why I'm calling. I'm trying to figure out what to do next, and I thought of you. Do you have a bit?"

"Sure... for you, you bet. What's the hitch?"

"Well, I'm not sure actually. I've been following hunches and the like and, well, I feel like I'm stuck. I'm working at a club for kids here in Phoenix and I've realized that it's not for me. I've got a week to go on my two weeks notice, and I've found a gal I'm interested in. She's going to med school in Tucson, though, and that's a couple of hours away. I also still haven't formally called things off with my kind of wife, Melinda. I know it's not meant to be, with her I mean, and, well, I flip flop." Brian let out a sigh. "It's kind of a mess really."

"Well, I hear that. I had an old friend say once that, 'All you can do is one thing at a time.' Once you get past that, you get into trouble."

"What do you mean?"

"Well, it sounds like you've got a lot of fear going on because you can't figure things out," he chuckled. "I know that one myself. Anyway, you can't do more than what's in front of you, 'one thing at a time,' so stop worrying. I know that's kind of blunt, but it's what I mean."

Breathe.

Click.

"Huh. That makes sense... it's just that things are so out of control, I mean, it's not life and death, but it sure feels like it is."

"This is gonna sound weird, Brian. I mean it's been a long time and, well, we've lost touch."

"Yeah."

"Well, what's your belief on how life works?"

"What do you mean?"

"Do you believe there's a force, or source for good in the world – in your world? In your life?" he paused. "It could be anything."

"I guess so," he paused. "Well, not really. I'm used to doing things all by myself."

"I believe you. That's partly my point. It doesn't matter what you 'believe' in. I think it's important for us to think that we aren't all alone, that there's something out there advocating for us - that wants us to be happy. The idea of everything being random, well, it doesn't work for me. It only fed my desire to do things all by myself."

I'm not following, Peter… can you break it down for me? Go ahead, be blunt… and, are you wearing a fedora?" he laughed.

"Nope," he started laughing, too. "What I mean is, when I used to do things on my own I would force and push things. It was the fear. My life looked great on the outside, it sucked for me on the inside, though. I was miserable… fear was running my life. I was forcing pretty much everything I touched. I was really afraid, Brian, do you see?"

"Not yet," he said. "Afraid of what?" he asked.

"You ask good questions," Peter chuckled. "Afraid I wasn't enough, that I wasn't worth being helped, advocated for or having the things I truly wanted. I was so used to being the 'lone wolf,' and all living that way really did was reinforce my fears. It was a self-fulfilling prophecy, really.

"Once I realized there was something else on my side, something out there helping me, well, I let up quite a bit." He chuckled, "I stopped chasing all those 'mini fears' that showed up each day. Honestly, I don't know that it matters if there is something else out there, really. I think it is important to have a sense of not being in your life, alone. What's true is, once I eased up, my life improved dramatically. My fear level dropped and things started falling into place. Things happened in ways I could never have planned.

"Brian, the key was that I had to let go of my fears first. It wasn't easy to begin with, but believing that something else was out there, on my side, well, it helped me with that."

Fear started to grow inside of Brian, it started from the bottom of his feet and worked its way up to his head. He started to sweat and his stomach churned. His forehead was damp and waves of warmth started to cover his entire body. It was as if he was afraid he'd been doing things wrong - that he'd made a major mistake.

After a few seconds, it let up a bit.

"What you're basically saying is to let go of trying to figure things out?"

"Yes, that's it Brian. Exactly. It can be challenging, I know, but it works out for the better. Trust me."

"Thanks Peter, you've been a big help. Thanks."

"You bet, Brian. Anytime."

As the words came out of his mouth, he knew Peter was right.

It occurred to Brian that when he lived like the old man and Peter had suggested; when he didn't force things, his life ran better. It was easier. Yes, it had taken quite a few turns, but his life was much better than before.

Guilt started to form, bubbling up from the bottom, like a hot tub.

> *Life is supposed to be a struggle.*

> *I have to work hard, I have to overcome things to be worthy of what I get.*

> *Who am I to just 'allow' and receive?*

Where did that come from?

Brian flashed back to a meeting with the old man. "You're fighting against years, centuries, even millennia's of beliefs here, Brian. Know that old habits, old beliefs, they die hard. We're engrained to suffer and struggle to get what we want. When you change things, when you change what you believe, well, there's bound to be resistance."

He realized that much of his previous life had been in response to his fears. Micro Tech, his wife, living in Redmond… the Range Rover. He had been living a life based out of fear, of making decisions to abate it. Once he smoothed one fear over, another fear would come right in and take its place. It's like he had a belief that he needed the fear in order to matter, to exist. It was a never ending string of fear, of 'micro' and 'macro' fears and the decisions to abate them. Each day, week and month were made of responding to and trying to abate his fears. He had been swimming in a never ending river of fear, fighting against the ebbs and flows.

Click.

I'll bet that's why the fears have been coming up unannounced.

My brain is probably afraid, he laughed. *Afraid that I won't need it anymore.*

Funny. It's afraid that it's not running my life anymore. That I know, he laughed.

Bingo.

Okay, so now that this is cleared up…what's next?

Oh yea, dinner with Tammie. His heart leapt in his chest.

Interesting, very interesting…

Right about 1:30, he got a call from Tina. She'd heard back that her girlfriend's husband, Travis. He'd okayed Brian coming to his school next week to help out. Volunteering was the next thing on his plate.

A wave of fear crept in. It started in his toes, worked its way through his stomach, through his chest and stopped at the top of his head. For a brief second, he felt like he couldn't move, like his body was inert.

Interesting.

The fear was followed by:

> *What the hell am I doing? A baseball coach? There's no money in that.*
>
> *And what about retirement and Tammie? She doesn't want to be with a coach.*
>
> *She's moving to Tucson. How's that going to work?*

He chuckled and took a deep breath. His heart was pounding and, flipping here and there in his chest and his ribcage felt stiff. Freaky stiff.

Oddly, he had a new presence about him. A part of him knew he was fine. This part seemed stronger than the part that felt alone and afraid. It was almost as if the stronger part of him was being a loving parent to a young, scared boy.

He decided to go for a walk, that would give him some relief and clarity. Right then, he thought about his real dad's flask and for a millisecond, the craving for a drink presented itself. He was able to watch it, to be present with the urge, and the urge left.

Interesting.

He went to his favorite spot downtown and started walking around. Brian realized he didn't feel like he was completely in his body. The feeling was much like the one from a few days ago, right before the car almost hit him. As he was walking, he saw the old man sitting on a bench near a coffee shop. He wasn't whistling.

This might be a serious one, Brian chuckled.

He walked over and sat next to him. The old man broke the silence. "Fear is interesting, Brian. Have you noticed… it's not intelligent?"

"What do you mean?"

"Have you noticed that whenever you confront your fears, when you really look at them, they're just smoke and mirrors? How there's very little truth in them."

"When you put it that way, yes." He flashed back to how afraid he'd gotten earlier in the day, how immobilized he was. During that time, he'd totally forgotten that Tina was checking in to him volunteering at the high school. He'd forgotten about all the good things happening in his life.

"You see, you can only focus on one thing at a time."

Brian laughed out loud, "You're right on, Old Man. Right on."

"It takes patience and compassion to work this, Brian. Remember, you're learning a new way of doing things. It's going to feel a bit uncomfortable for a while." He took a breath. "Nothing happens that you aren't able to handle, and sometimes we need help. Never be afraid to ask."

Brian took a deep breath. He was so hard on himself.

"Compassion is the bridge to make this work. If you're hard on yourself, all you do is give the fear more ammunition. Judgment and criticism are the cousins of fear. They're just obstacles to who you really are."

With a hug and a tug of his fedora, the old man was off again.

Brian sat there, feeling waterlogged and a bit logy from all the new information. The good news was that his head was still above the water line.

His night had been non-eventful, mainly because his brain had shut off, much like a circuit breaker in a house. His brain was overloaded and flat out shut off.

No power. No buzzing. Zip. Nada.

7

He woke up abruptly at 6:45 a.m..

Who?

His forehead was drenched with sweat.

"Who?" he said out loud.

Another wave of fear started, this time in his chest. It moved through his body and lodged there, like a loaf of lead molasses. His body was tingly.

Mom, no. Dad, dunno where he is. Stepdad, dead.

Breathe.

"What is going on!?" He was yelling to an empty apartment.

As weird as it sounded, he decided to go for a run.

Yes, a run.

It was a long one today. He started out at the usual place and at his usual pace. Within the first few minutes, he noticed something profound: The more he thought about his problems, the more stressed out he got. Literally, he started to feel sick to his stomach when he followed the path of his thinking. At one point, he became so nauseous that he had to stop.

Taking deep breaths, Brian envisioned the large safe that had worked earlier. He placed all the fears that were showing up during his run safely inside. He heard the old man's voice say: "What you focus on gets bigger. Brian, you can only focus on one thing at a time."

He closed the safe and heard the loud "thud" of the poles slamming into the steel frame. He started thinking and envisioning what he wanted: A loving wife, a wonderful home, children and a career that he loved deeply.

He wanted to be happy, live in joy and feel fulfilled. He wanted to love and be loved, deeply.

As he focused on this, as he put them in his mind, he generated the feeling of having them. Not the sense of accomplishment, rather the feeling of actually having the things he wanted, of their being in the here and now.

The fear shifted, like molten lava, it moved out of his body leaving a warm path behind. He started his run up again. He realized there was hope.

What a trip! he thought.

Whether there was something greater than him or not, he realized that if he acted out of a fear place - out of thinking he needed to do something because he was afraid - that thinking took him away from creating what he wanted.

"Fear can never be trusted," the old man said. "Your brain can be a friend or ally. You choose. You choose, Kiddo."

He continued his run, finding the wonderful rhythm that he enjoyed. After a few minutes, he glanced up to see a gigantic billboard across the valley. It said, "What wolf are you going to feed?"

Click.

He laughed to himself.

Perfect.

Whichever wolf I pay attention to, Joy or Suffering, Love or Fear, Failure or Hope, Abandonment or Trust, that's the one that will get bigger. So, do I want to create the life I want or do I want to live in fear?

He kept up his run and worked on not thinking while allowing the insights to happen. He got how his fear started when he tried to figure things out. It was like the adrenaline and cortisone switch was flipped in his body.

When he wasn't thinking of positive, heart and hope filled things, when he was in fear, the 'fear rabbit' would start its run in its little hamster cage and nothing good really came out of it. He soon realized that the more he focused on what he wanted, on what made his heart sing, the happier he got.

Lesson learned, Old Man. Lesson learned.

He decided he would give the old man a big hug the next time he saw him. He finished up his run, absorbing the beauty of his surroundings and the crisp, fresh air.

He went back to his rig, got his towel and some water from inside and started his cool down routine. Out of the corner of his eye, he saw the old man walking to him. It brought a smile to Brian's face.

The old man walked up and said, "How are you doing, Son?"

"I'm great." Brian paused and said, "Well, not so great, but great. Do you know what I mean?" Brian remarked.

The old man chuckled, "I think so, Brian. I think so," he paused. "Well," he laughed, "I felt a tremor in the force, so I thought I would show up."

"Thanks," Brian said, and he walked up to the Old Man and gave him a big hug. "Thank you," he said.

"Oh, shoot. I'm all sweaty. Sorry."

"No worries, Brian. You're good. I get it."

"I've been dealing with quite a bit of fear of late, at night and during the day, it's been quite a pain, really. I'm not used to it."

"I see," the Old Man said. "Well, you might consider that you're not used to the new way you're doing things, that's what's causing the fear."

"Huh?"

"Remember, old energy dies hard, Brian, and it takes courage, compassion and time to move through it. It takes time." He added, "It's like the old part of you is dying and it's taking some last gasps at keeping you where you were, do you see?"

"I guess. You mean kind of like I'm fighting a battle and it knows its lost, so it's taking some wild shots."

"Yes, exactly, except I wouldn't use the war idea. If you fight back you're actually in the same old energy again, it's like you're using your fear to fight your fear. You'd be in the same old energy that you're fighting."

Brian's face was as blank as his brain.

The old man smiled. "Let me put it another way. It's like your brain doesn't want you to change, it wants to continue to control your life, so it's creating all this fear. If you look at it, all the things you're afraid of are brain generated, either through beliefs of losing or not gaining something, or of other non-reality based ideas and concepts.

"The truth is, everything is okay. You're doing great and your brain is, well, freaking out a bit." The old man placed a reassuring hand on Brian's shoulder.

"If you fight back with fear, you're in the same energy. You actually feed it."

"I don't quite get it yet," Brian said. "I'll sit with it though. I know I'll get it."

"Remember, your life conspires for your success."

"What?"

"Your life conspires for your success.

"Don't think lack or scarcity. Know that there are people, places and things conspiring for you to succeed. As long as you're open to receive and you focus on the positive, on what you want and live your life from that place - you'll create that exact thing."

"Yea, but what about the days I'm in fear, when I can't hold it?"

"Don't worry, Brian, you're human. Do your best. Don't let the idea of perfection get in the way of good enough."

"What?" Brian asked.

"Don't let perfection get in the way of good enough. Keep trying, you don't have to be perfect. Your life answers back to your predominant thoughts. It's like carbon copy paper."

"Like what?"

"Carbon copy paper."

Brian had a quizzical look on his face. He shook his head and said, "Old man, you're downloading a lot."

"I know," he said. "It's all in there, Brian," he laughed. "Trust me. Your brain wants you to think you'll forget. Have you noticed you remember when the time is right?"

"Now that you mention it… yes."

"Back to carbon copy paper," the old man laughed. "Well, it's like this. Whatever thoughts you put out, your life replicates. Have you ever gotten up in an awful space, thinking your day would be a drag?"

"Yea, sure."

"Well, how did your day go?"

"It was awful"

"Bingo.

"Your life cares enough about you to give you exactly what you are wanting."

"But, I'm not wanting a crappy day."

"Well, according to your thinking, you were. You were expecting it even."

Click.

"Wait, are you saying I need to micromanage my thinking?"

"No, not so much micromanage, Brian, become more aware of it. You'll get what your predominant thoughts are, see? But wait, there's more if you want."

"Sure, what's that?"

"If you really want to make things happen, create the feeling of what you want along with your thoughts, then, keep them in tune. And, even to amp it up more, say them out loud, too."

"What?"

"Your life is like a receiver, Brian. It replicates what you generate. It's like when you played as a kid, remember how vivid and alive it felt? The more input you give it, the more it generates. Thoughts, feelings and what you say out loud - your voice - are the vehicles that connect to the receiver. Get it?"

"Well, yes, I guess," he paused. "Wait, no. This is kind of scaring me a bit. What if I have negative thoughts?"

"I have a question, Brian. Is this you talking, or the fear from your brain?"

Brian hesitated and sat with it for a few seconds. "Ah, it's my fear Old Man, my fear."

"Okay, now, sit with what I said, not from the fear place. The good news too, is that all fear does is manifest more fear. People used to think that being in fear would create the thing that you're afraid of. That's not true anymore. Nope, all it does now is snowball the feeling. It can manifest negative things because you're not on track or delay positive things, but it's a minor side effect. It's nothing to worry about or be afraid of," he laughed.

Click.

"Got it. It's not that my life wants to give me the hard stuff, it wants me to succeed. It will give me negative things if I focus on them quite a bit, yet the only reason it does it is to help me discern if I really want them."

"Right!" the old man grinned.

"Wait," Brian laughed. "There's more! By getting the negative I also realize even more how much I don't want it. So, no matter what happens, I win."

"Now you're cooking, Kiddo, now you're cooking!" the old man said. "Live your life, to the best of your ability, free of fear. All you do is show up, do what really needs to be done, not more, and know what you're wanting and things will start happening.

"Think about what you've done so far, Brian. You started to listen to your life, you had a deep knowing to leave Micro Tech and you did. Look at what you're creating Brian, how it's unfolding - and you're just getting started.

"Remember, your adversary, your own worst enemy is your brain. It creates fear at a drop of a hat. That fear creates ripples that affect your day, week, decades and even future generations. It's not that it creates the things you're afraid of in your life, it's that it creates and spirals more fear. Sometimes, it shows up in your body and immobilizes you. You see, all that fear gets transferred to each other if nobody wakes up. Have you noticed how you feel when everyone starts talking about what their afraid of? How people spiral and worry, especially in groups? It gets out of hand and negative really fast. Sometimes, it's like quicksand."

"Yeah, my brain creates more fear and, well, it doesn't feel real good."

"Exactly! Brian, you can control your reality, you can change your fate, your lot in life. You are the master of your own ship."

Cachunk.

Brian flashed back to his drowning ship nightmare and realized how he had changed his life, and his dream, because of the new, loving choices he made for himself. He remembered how he learned his self-esteem was so attached to his mom and dad's opinion, how he forgot who he was.

He instantly got:

> You are who you choose to be.
>
> You don't need to be driven by your past.
>
> You're not your current situation or circumstance. You're much more than that.

As Brian changed his beliefs, his thoughts changed, then his feelings, then the dreams, and then his life. They were all connected.

Brain said, "I get it. I didn't believe I was worthy of being helped, that I was good enough, so, I forced my way through life. I didn't believe I was worthy of good things, of a nice life, of being happily married and doing a job I loved. I thought, no, wait... I believed I wasn't good enough."

The old man leaned back, smiling and nodded softly.

Memories started flooding back and Brian became a young boy again. His dad said, "You have to work hard to get anywhere in life, Brian." His mom said, "Get them before they get you. Don't trust anyone Brian. They all want something. Watch your back."

Tears started welling up as he remembered his mom telling him when he was seven, "You don't want to be a doctor, Brian. Remember what Jerry said: 'Work hard and a man can achieve anything.' Mommy wants you to retire when you're young. You don't want to be a doctor. People sue doctors, Brian. You don't want that Brian. Not you. Not my son."

A knot formed in his stomach. It slowly grew into a ten pound loaf of bread made out of lead, pure, heavy, grey lead. It tasted awful. The warmth from this 'bread' branched out into his body, and the tears started to flow. He grabbed a napkin, preparing himself for what was coming.

You see, a lid had been taken off the vat of years of stuffed emotions, truths, inner knowings and passions. This lid was made up of learned beliefs and thoughts that were, in fact, untrue. It was painted with: "Everything is fine, just fine" and it was sealed shut with: "Even if something doesn't feel right, that I know isn't me, I'll do it, say it and be it anyway."

Flowing out from inside him were decades of true feelings, feelings from ignoring what he wanted, of placating to his mom's hidden and spoken needs and adapting to what his mom and dad wanted. Each time he stuffed more and more into his vat, the vat that ran his life, the vat that took him away from his truth, each time he stuffed things into his vat, the farther away he got from who he really was, and is.

Anger started to take him over. It was overwhelming. He felt like smacking someone, anyone... anything. The rage grew. If he wasn't in public, he would have screamed and done that very thing.

The old man interrupted the silence. "Breathe, Brian, breathe. I can see the anger welling up inside you. It's okay to acknowledge it, to move it, to let it go. Don't play with it though, it will ruin you if you do. Let it go, Brian. Let it go."

Brian released his anger and let it go. Like a lead filled balloon full of years of anger and rage, the anger left his chest, headed up into the air and disappeared behind the wispy clouds that filled the bright blue sky. What remained on earth was a wrung out man that felt forty pounds lighter. He felt like a cleaned out fish, leaving only room for the truth of who he was. There was room for the authentic Brian to return.

A soft voice welled up from inside him. It was as if someone was whispering it into his ear.

"Be true to yourself, Brian. It's okay now. Be true to you. You're safe."

He exhaled amidst tears. It took more effort than normal, it was like he was under water.

A doctor. A coach? A coaching doctor. Silly.

The old man broke the silence.

"That's the ticket, Kiddo… you're getting it." He paused, " How are you doing?"

Brian wiped the tears from his face with a napkin. He was getting pretty used to the coarseness, now. The breaths, the sobs were getting easier. He felt laughter creeping up from inside.

"I'm good, Old Man. I'm good." Brian started to laugh. "Wow. Who knew?"

"Great, that's all for today. You've got this, Kiddo, you've got this."

"You're on a schedule," Brian interrupted with a smile.

The old man laughed, "Yes, I'm on a schedule." He smiled, winked and started down the road.

Brian decided to look into being a physician. He was scared, but not in fear like before. He was scared because it was new. He'd wanted to be a doctor ever since he was a kid. He knew it in his bones.

The next morning he woke easily. He felt like a new man, lighter, with purpose and passion again. He cooked himself a light breakfast, ate and found some paper… some yellow paper.

He sat at the table and thought over the meetings he'd had with the old man. A smile came to his face along with some of the important things he'd learned. He titled the page, "Truths about Living."

1. Your brain can be your greatest enemy

2. Fear isn't smart and can never be trusted

3. What you fight against gets bigger

4. Everything happens for a reason

5. The universe wants you to be happy

6. Your life colludes for your success

7. Do what's in front of you, not from a place of worry or fear

8. What you focus on gets bigger

Feeling rather accomplished and knowing that his life was just beginning, he got his running gear, changed and headed out for his morning run. He repeated these phrases as he ran, in cadence with his breath. He felt rejuvenated and full of life. He felt hope and a deep knowing and connection with everything. It was as if he was filling up the very space that had been emptied out in the last meeting with the old man. He was filling up with hope, dreams, ease and joy. The good stuff. He felt more and more like his true self.

As he was running, he heard the old man's voice say: "Everything happens for a reason. Something good will come out of this."

Later that night he pulled up at Marko's to meet Tammie. It was a bit before seven. He sat in his rig and took a few minutes to slow down, to be.

He appreciated and was proud of all the changes he had been making. A smile came to his face, he'd come such a long way. His heart opened up and started to feel warm. Tears started to form as he realized how grateful he was; grateful to be on this path, for the people that had helped him and for the courage he had to make the changes. He kept smiling as he left his rig and went inside. Tammie was just inside the door, waiting.

She looked gorgeous. He pecked her on the cheek, they hugged and Brian's heart warmed. They found a table and he pulled out a chair for her. He sat down, smiling.

"How are things?" he asked.

"Good... you?" They both laughed.

"So, when is your last day at the club?" she asked.

"Friday."

"How are you doing with that?"

"I'm good. I forgot for a while that 'Everything happens for a reason,' it's all part of the journey. I reverted to panic mode a bit."

"Panic?"

"Yea, all of a sudden my brain was like: 'Stop. What are you doing? You have no clue where you're going,'" he laughed. "I forgot to 'Not believe everything I think.'"
There was an awkward pause. "Say," she said, "Can we talk about us for a minute?"

Clank.

"Sure." He felt a knot in his stomach.

"I like you a lot Brian, I just don't see us going anywhere."

Clank.

A part of him wanted to argue, yet he knew that if he needed to convince her now, he'd repeat that pattern over and over and over again. The fact was, if it was meant to be, it would. Forcing things into something it wasn't, well, never works out.

"I mean, I'm off to med school and you are on your own journey, you know?"

It was like Brian's brain tripped back in time. He instantly saw himself talking to the first gal he dated in high school. She had done pretty much the same thing, with different circumstances. Tears started to form and he had to snap himself back to the present.

"Bummer, and okay," he said. "I understand. Friends it is." His heart ached a bit and it felt like a little door closed inside him. He knew this was for the best and that if she was a 'no,' it left room for a 'yes' from the right one.

It still hurt, though. Not a profound, life ending hurt like he felt before, this was more of a sadness that she wasn't it, that the hope he had for her was over.

"You're okay with this?"

"Well, if it's not meant to be, forcing it will, well, it'll just make it worse."

She let out a sigh. "Ok, good. I was afraid you'd take it differently."

Odd, he thought. There was a twinge in her voice, similar to his mom's when she was trying to guilt him.

God, I'm glad I can see things like this now.

"No worries, it's all good," he added.

He felt the sensation of a door closing in front of him, shutting the opportunity with Tammie. He felt relieved, actually.

Interesting, he thought.

He heard a thought come through him:

> *Go with the flow. Know that what you desire is coming to you. As a matter of fact it's already there. All you need to do is show up, know and explore. Easy.*

Interesting.

They engaged in pleasant small talk for the rest of the dinner and split the check. He gave her a hug and they went their separate ways.

"Good luck," he said.

"You, too!"

He exhaled and noticed his brain was going to a funky place. He felt a pull to go to a place of, "It'll never happen" and "Why me?" The fact was, he knew the universe was on his side. This just meant that Tammie wasn't for him, that's all. His brain wanted to globalize, to make it: "It'll never happen," and "Woe is me."

> *No, I'm not going there. I know that what I want, and what I desire is already there.*
>
> *I don't need to suffer, to worry or stress. All I need to do is focus, keep my eye on the ball and keep showing up.*

Easy peasy.

Brian went home, tossed his keys on the counter and started to think about how fortunate he was. Yes, he felt a sadness about his hopes with

Tammie not working out. He also knew the right woman was out there, she was coming.

Now, some of you may be thinking he should "fight" for her. The thing is, when you do this, well, it never works out - it usually only clouds things up for a while. It often just prolongs the agony.

He remembered a meeting with the old man. "Once you have to convince someone, then they have to 'stay' convinced. This means you change, or do things you don't really want to, in hopes that they don't leave.

"Look for mutual attraction and connection, a woman that's strong, clear, that knows who she is, what she wants and has the strength to stay true to herself... like you.

"If you don't, you'll be on a carnival ride. It'll be fun in a way, for a while. Up and down, up and down, but ultimately the ride ends and a part of you knows the whole time that it was a ride, that it wasn't real. Wait for something real to show up. You'll know Brian. You'll know. I'm not saying it'll be instantaneous, it may grow like it did with my wife, Wanda. Listen to yourself, Brian. Trust yourself. You'll know."

He had the courage to do what was right with his mom, to know what he needed to do with his estranged wife, Melinda, and what do with his career and his life. His path was becoming clearer. He didn't need to be somebody he wasn't and he didn't need to be what his mom or dad wanted him to be. He was free to be who he really was and to create what he truly wanted. He was free to discover what truly fulfilled him.

"I'm one lucky dude!" he said aloud.

He flicked on the TV and an episode of Gilligan's Island was on. Gilligan was telling the Skipper, "Don't believe everything you think."

"How is that possible?" the Skipper asked.

"Well, think of how often your brain wants to argue with you. It wants to tell you that you aren't good enough, that you're a jerk, that you have to work harder and more than anyone else to prove to others that you're... wait for it... 'worthy.' What we forget is that we are all worthy. Actually, that 'forgetting' is what gets us in trouble. We forget who we are and then end up in the funniest places, like here, on this island."

Gilligan, dropping knowledge on the Skipper.

Funk. Funk.

Huh, that's what happened earlier. I started to get into a funk. It was triggered by a feeling, I think.

Wait.

Brian recognized that there was a subtle, soft, quiet thought a millisecond before the feeling.

It was just a fraction of a second.

He realized that while he was watching TV, a thought had popped into his head, right before the feeling.

The thought that: *I will never find her.*

Right after that, the pit of his stomach flipped and he had a twinge in his stomach that swept through his entire torso. The twinge was fear.

The image of a calm and peaceful pond appeared in his mind, a calm pond that had a large rock dropped in it. The initial splash disrupted everything and the ripples lasted for quite some time.

Click.

The thought, even though it was brief, was like a rock being dropped into the calmness of his mind. It was magnified by his focusing on the rock, that's what made it more real, more intense. Truthfully, a part of him believed the fear, or else the rock would not have appeared, or if it had, it would have had no effect.

You see, thoughts that bug us often contain a fear that we have, or else we would instantly shrug it off – it wouldn't bother us.

Your thoughts create your reality.

> *So, this thought created ripples and the ripples created feelings that lead to the sadness and the funk.*
>
> *A funk that I got out of when I told myself the truth.*
>
> *The truth is, Tammie isn't a fit and the right woman is on her way.*

Brian smiled.

Man, we are amazing creatures, he laughed.

He wondered, too, if this is a variation of what the old man meant when he said, "What you focus on gets bigger."

Interesting.

A feeling crept in at that point, a feeling and remembering that he hadn't been to a bookstore in a while.

I'll go tomorrow, after my run.

His night started off well, he fell asleep easily and peacefully, then a dream crept in. It was the dream of him drowning on a ship again, as a boy. The one where he, his mom and step-dad boarded the Deep Insight and he drowned. He woke up dripping in sweat. It was like he had drowned and died, again.

What the…?

He looked around, got his bearings of when and where he was, and got up. He ambled into the kitchen and poured himself a glass of water.

"Everything happens for a reason," he'd heard the old man say.

"Well great, Old Man. Great! Now what?" he laughed.

I can choose to make this hard and fight it, or allow it to be easy.

I choose ease.

Life can be as easy or as hard as you make it.

He decided to journal for a bit. It felt like the right thing to do. He grabbed some paper, and a pen, and sat down at his kitchen table.

Go with the flow, he thought to himself. *What the hell, another damn dream?*

Wait. Ok. Another dream.

Why? Why?

He looked at the paper for a few minutes. It was still blank when he laughed.

Okay, well, so this is passive journaling.

He kept looking at the paper. "The dreams are happening for a reason. Why?" he asked himself.

He started to write:

> The dream is trying to tell me something. The funks are happening because I'm focusing on the problem, I'm focusing on how I don't have something. Focusing on that is leading me down the wrong path. If I continue with this I'll be living my life out of fear again. I'll be doing things to placate, to take care of the fear like I did before. Fear will be woven into the fabric of my life. That's not how I want to live. I am no longer willing to live that way.
>
> Remember that fear is not intelligent, it can't be trusted and abundance is a state of being from which everything comes.
>
> Notice the past tense.
>
> I now choose to live out of love, out of joy, life, passion, purpose, prosperity and knowing that my life, my life is colluding for my success.   All I merely need to do is to listen. Listen, Brian. Listen. Create your life from that place, from the knowing of who I am.

Listen, Brian.

Listen.

The phone rang. It was the old man.

How did he get my number?

Interesting.

"You're doing well, Brian. You're getting quite a bit. Nice."

"What do you mean?"

"You're putting the pieces together, that's wonderful." He paused briefly, "You had the boat dream again, didn't you?"

"Yes. How did you know?"

"No worries, Brian, I just know. So, what do you think it means? The dream, I mean?"

"I'm not..." he heard himself say. He'd stopped mid-sentence.

Wait. I do know. Watch what I say... I am listening.

"Hang on for a second," he paused and took a breath.

"Having the dream means I'm forcing things and it's showing me that what I think actually shows up in my life. At the least, it shows up as feelings and at the most, situations or circumstances."

"Good. Very good, Brian. So, what's next?"

"What's next is I buy you dinner..." he laughed. "Seriously, I'm going to go back to sleep knowing that my good, the job, the woman, my purpose, my life is already made and done the way I want it.   I'm going to know that all I need to do is to show up and receive it. To be grateful, to know it and receive it."

"Good, Brian. Good. Remember, your brain can be an adversary. Don't believe everything you think." he paused. "Good night, Brian."

"Good night, Old Man."

What a trip.

8

He woke up the next morning wondering how much of last night was a dream and how much actually happened. He saw that his journal was out on the table, he flipped through it and found the comments he wrote from last night along with what the old man had said on the phone.

Well, okay then, he laughed. *What's next?*

 He picked up his journal and wrote:

> What I do know is: It's going to be a great day. Life is for me, never against me. I'm on the right track!

He went to the club, a little nervous since it was Friday, his last day. He parked, took a deep breath and glanced at the 3 x 5 card on his dash before he went inside. He took a few extra moments to really look and remember the place, the situations and the kids.

It was like he was taking pictures in his mind so he could remember. It wasn't that he didn't like it here, it was that it just wasn't a fit, it wasn't his purpose. He knew that he didn't lose track of time here. There were some aspects that were okay, and he knew there was no "perfect" job, yet in the bigger picture he knew it wasn't for him. He felt sad about the kids, about Tabitha. He'd miss them, and her.

He clocked in, said hello to William and walked into the homework room. In the back corner was Tabitha, studying away. He walked over and said hello.

"Hey," she said. "So, it's your last day, huh?"

"Yes, yes it is."

"Well," she said. "I want you to know that I really appreciated your help," she sighed. "You were a big influence for me, and not just with the math.

I appreciate that you showed me how to not give up, to believe in myself. So….thanks, Mr. Richardson."

"You're welcome. You helped me, you know?"

"Whaaat?" she laughed.

"Yup. By hanging out with you, I actually heard what I was saying… it changed me, too."

They high fived. It was a good day. At the end of his last day with William and the Boys and Girls Club, he clocked out, shook William's hand, thanked him and headed back to his apartment.

Later, he made himself a nice dinner. He grilled a thin steak, some veggies and a nice salad. He was excited. Tomorrow he would be showing up to practice to see about coaching. He felt a twang in his stomach, like he knew it wasn't a fit.

I'm going to show up anyway.

The next day he showed up, right on time. He knew as he walked up to the school that this wasn't it. He made an agreement, though, and out of respect to Tina, Travis and himself, he honored it. Besides, you never know. Brian was learning how to work with his intuition. You never know what might happen.

"Hi, Travis."

"Hi, Brian. I'm glad you're here," Travis said as they shook hands.

"Come on back." Travis gave him a tour of the locker room. Brian remembered the good old days of playing ball in high school. It brought a smile to his face.

Travis took him to the playing field where the kids were warming up, doing drills.

Man, I love this smell. The grass, the fresh air.

Brian lit up as memories started flooding in, good ones. He loved baseball. He loved the sense of accomplishment from the game and how everyone worked together as a team. One time, while he was playing in the outfield, he saw clear as a bell how right as the ball was pitched, the entire outfield took a small step at the same time. It was magical for him.

The game, for Brian, was spiritual really. Whenever he played, he lost all sense of time. He loved how a game could go on forever. The smell of the grass, the smell his mitt had when he put his nose inside it and took a whiff. Tears formed.

I love this game…

He spent the day with the kids and the coach. He felt good, sharing and teaching tidbits he'd learned from his playing days. It felt good. As he watched practice, he noticed there was a young boy in the outfield struggling a bit.

They were running situational drills with base runners and he was having a hard time with the throws in from the outfield, he wasn't regularly hitting the cutoff man. He also was having some problems with catching pop flies. It looked like he did fine on most balls, yet he had challenges with the routine "can o' corn," the high pop ups.

He asked Travis if he could chat with him for a few minutes.

"Bobby? Sure," he said. "We've tried some things with him, nothing seems to stick, though."

You see, Bobby reminded Brian of himself growing up, he had similar problems. He trotted out to the young man and said hello.

"Hi," Bobby said.

"Hi," Brian said.

"Say, I'm noticing you're having a hard time with a couple things. Would you like some ideas?"

"No, I got this," he chirped. "Who are you, anyway?"

"I'm Brian," he said. "Nobody special. I went through some similar things when I was playing, about your age, actually. That's all." Brian smiled, turned and started to trot off.

"Hey, Mister," Bobby said. "Wait."

Brian stopped and turned around. "Sure, what's up?"

Bobby motioned him over with his glove. "I would actually."

"Would what?"

"Like some ideas, okay?"

"Sure. I was just messing with you," Brian smiled. He trotted back.

"When? With the ideas or just now?"

"Just now." They both laughed.

"Okay, Old Man. What you got?"

"The trick is to focus on the moment."

A blank look showed up on Bobby's face. The look was high definition, Technicolor in Dolby Digital sound.

"Let me say it in a different way."

"Please."

"When you see the pop ups, and there's tons of time, do you notice yourself thinking about the ball, about tripping or dropping it."

"Yup," he said with a heavy emphasis on the "p." He made a popping sound when he said it.

"Well, that's called worrying or 'future tripping.' Until you gain confidence in knowing you've got it, try talking to yourself out loud, or sing a song. Do something to occupy your mind, give it something to do in the quiet time."

"Okay, cool. There's this one song by Heavy D I like, cool."

"Great. Now, what's going on with you hitting your cutoff man? I can tell you know you need to, but your ball is doing weird stuff."

"Yeah, I can't figure that one out. One time I chucked it in and it broke left over second base. The dang thing landed in the dugout." Bobby had a look of disgust on his face.

"Awesome," Brian chuckled.

"What?" Bobby looked a bit offended.

"Awesome. That means you've got a great arm. Was it on a rope?"

"You bet. It was hecka cool actually. The entire infield was looking at me like, whaaat?!"

"Cool," Brian said. "Show me how you held it."

Bobby showed him. He had his first and second finger across the two closest seams.

"Mine used to do weird stuff, too. Try this." Brian showed him how to hold the ball across the two widest seams. "It's what pitchers call a four seamer. When I did this, it wouldn't bank left or right anymore. It might sail a bit on me at times, but it was always on a straight line. See?"

Brian called out to the second basemen, getting his attention. With the ball in his left hand, Brian simulated a catch. He raised his left hand in the air, started to crow hop towards second base. He brought his left hand across his chest and transferred the ball to his right hand. Still moving, he finished the crow hop and launched the ball right at the second baseman, all in one fluid motion. "See?"

"Yea, Old Man. That was awesome. So, what's up with your arm motion? It looks weird."

"Well, I learned this when I had some arm stiffness. It helped get rid of it, plus I could put more on the throw. I forget what it's called. For me, when I throw this way, though, I get more lat, torso and lower body involved - plus I come over the top more. That's what keeps it straight, I think," he paused, noticing Bobby was nodding his head. "Try it."

Bobby tried it a couple of times. With a few minor adjustments, he had it.

"You're a quick study, Kiddo. You got it."

"Thanks, Old Man. Thanks!"

"You bet, anytime," Brian started to trot into the infield. He paused, turned to Bobby and said, "One more thing. Trust, don't think!"

Bobby, nodded, smiled and held up his mitt as if to high five. Brian turned and headed into the coach's dugout.

"Trust, don't think." I have to take my own advice.

Believe in yourself and that you can. That I can.

After a few hours, that felt like minutes, Travis called practice. He brought everyone in and reviewed some of the concepts from the drills. He also gave them a bit of a pep talk.

"Believe," Travis said, "Don't think. Believe in yourself. Skills can be learned. Trust, have fun and keep coming back!" He clapped his hands, "Okay, that's it for today. See you tomorrow, 'Same bat time, same bat channel!' Bring it in!"

The entire team circled around him, putting their hands towards the center.

"Middleton on three," he yelled. The kids pumped their hands in unison with an up and down motion. They all yelled: "One, two, three – Middleton!"

Awesome!

The kids all headed into the locker room. The click of the spikes on the concrete brought a smile to Brian's face.

"So, what do you think? Do you want to help out?" Travis asked.

"I'd love to Travis. I'm not sure yet if this is my main thing, and I'd love to chip in here and there. Would that be okay?"

"You bet, I'd be glad to have you. I can tell you're great with kids, and Bobby sure improved. What did you tell him, by the way?"

"Not much, just some things I learned growing up."

"Well, it sure worked," he paused. "Let me know when you'd like to come back."

"You bet. Thanks, Travis."

They shook hands, and Brian headed to his rig and drove home. Brian knew he loved sports and that he loved hanging out with kids, he loved helping them. Knowing that, though, he felt stuck.

I wonder what's next.

He plopped on his sofa, put his feet on the table and took a breath. He chilled out for a few minutes, no thinking, just blank brain time. A phrase popped in his head, one that he'd learned recently.

The universe wants you to be happy.

Click.

He got up, went to his fridge and took the paper off it. As he looked at it, another phrase popped out at him:

Do what's in front of you, not from a place of worry or fear.

A sense of relief, and inner knowing, and a feeling of direction moved through him.

What's next?

What's next was a nice meal, a bit of journaling and bed. He slept wonderfully and woke up refreshed. He went for his run, grabbed breakfast and went to a nearby park to hang out.

As he pulled into the parking lot he noticed a bumper sticker on a car: "Don't believe everything you think." He laughed out loud. He went to a nearby bench and started watching the ducks. They were amazing. They didn't think, they did. They were in the moment.

I'll bet they don't worry, he chuckled.

He went for a walk of blankness, smiling from ear to ear. About halfway through, a thought popped into his head.

Doctor. Doctor. Doctor?

Why didn't I?

Click.

This was his next step. He knew it. He felt it deep down.

It was if his brain heard him making the connection, and immediately it kicked in like a back-up generator, and the fear followed:

> *Dang, I'll be thirty eight when I graduate and then three or four years of residency, minimum.*

> *I'll be an old man, in my forties. Geez!*

> *Then, there's the malpractice insurance… and doctors get sued all the time.*

Suddenly, he remembered the bumper sticker. "Don't believe everything you think."

Don't believe everything you think!

He laughed again.

Okay, okay I get it. I'm listening. He smiled.

Let's see. What's true? Yes, I will be thirty eight when I get out of school, maybe forty three when I start up a practice.

He felt the pull in his stomach.

What thought am I thinking that's creating this?

He sat and it occurred to him that he was thinking he was too old, that all that time would pass, and all that work, plus the enormous amount of and years of homework. Ugh!!!!

It was fear based thinking, plain and simple.

Hold on brain. Wait.

What's true?

> *Number 8: What you focus on gets bigger.*

> *Okay. I do want to be a doctor and it may take some time. I'm not going to future trip about the "homework," or the study.*

> *I want this, I can do it and I'm going to.*

He had a solid feeling come from within and it felt right. Then, other thoughts poured in.

> *What about the malpractice?*

Man, that felt heavy, he thought.

Where did that come from? Mom? Mom.

Okay, do I believe it?

He felt his stomach turn and he flat out felt off, again. This was a big moment for him and he knew it.

He felt his heart open and it heated up a bit. You see, he realized it wasn't about his mom or stepdad, they were doing the best they could. It was about loving that he was coming back to himself, his true self.

The truth was, he knew his childhood experiences and adult ones... Micro Tech, Melinda, all of that stuff, served a purpose. That's what got him here...to where, and who, he was today.

He also knew that fighting it, staying mired in it would only keep him from growing back into who he really was. His heart continued to grow warm. He wiped away the tears from his face.

He paused.

What's true?

Some will get sued, some won't. Just because others have that experience doesn't mean I will.

I am my own person, I'll have my own experience and I will not have fear run my life. I will trust.

His stomach calmed down and he felt refreshed - at ease. His heart seemed to vibrate now.

He remembered his talk with Peter: "You can't do more than what's in front of you, 'one thing at a time...'"

Click.

One step at a time. One step, one day, one month. Easy peasy. He woke up the next morning, refreshed, focused and knowing what his next step was - finding his medical school.

Around 11:30 that morning, his phone rang. It was Melinda, he swiped right.

"Hi, Brian."

"Hi, Melinda."

"How are you?" she asked.

"I'm good. You?"

"Good. Say, I was thinking of coming down to Phoenix and spending some time with you, what do you think?"

Brian felt a twinge in his stomach and a familiar pull to be with her again. He took a breath and remembered what he knew.... he knew they weren't a fit any longer.

"Melinda, it would be good to see you. I know it won't go past friendship for me, though. I care about you and I valued our time together, I just know that we aren't a fit."

"Are you sure? I miss, you," she said. He could tell that she was crying.

The twinge and pull again. Tears started to form.

Why is this so dang hard? he wondered.

It was because he was feeling again. He had learned as a boy to turn them off, to not be...to not be Brian. He learned to be only what was expected of him. Now, he was becoming fully alive again.

He knew, even amidst his feelings, that it was over for him with Melinda. He knew that ending it was the correct thing to do. "Yes, Melinda, I am sure. I do love you and I wish you the best. That door has closed in my life."

"Okay, Brian." He could still hear her crying. "Well, good luck to you."

"You too, Melinda. Goodbye."

Grief moved through his body and tears formed in his eyes. He felt a sense of completion inside when he told her. It was followed up with a deep ache. His heart, only a few moments ago, was aglow and vibrating. Now it ached and cracked like an egg over a frying pan, soon to be dropped into the deep warm heat.

He knew the feelings coming up were from the healthy grieving of the loss of hope of what might have been with her. His intuition told him that avoiding those feelings, that not wanting to feel them is what kept him from deciding earlier. He knew if he hadn't ended it now, it only would have prolonged the agony, the pain that was going to come anyway. It's what a lot of us do.

Brian refocused on knowing that when he closed that door, it left space for a person to take up that space. Ending it was what was best for him. He knew it and also knew it was important to have his grief. There was time with her that was great.

He focused on having his feelings, knowing this was part of making space for the right fit.

As the tears continued to flow, he pulled out his journal and wrote her a 'good bye' letter, one that he would never send. It was part of his closure, of his moving forward and embracing his life. After an hour or so, the grief started to shift.

He decided to try the new sandwich shop close to his place, Jim's Deli. He walked over, opened the door and no bell. Nothing. He ordered a turkey and ham sandwich on whole wheat with cheddar cheese. He grabbed a bag of chips, poured himself an orange soda and paid. He found a booth in the back and sat down.

He pulled open the bag of chips and took a whiff. As he peered up from the bag, he saw the old man walking over to him.

"Hi," Brian said.

"Hi, Son, how are you?" the old man asked as he slid into the booth.

"I'm kind of feeling like my life is a bit up in the air. I ended it with Melinda earlier today, and I've closed a couple of doors on relationships, and on career ideas - I'm feeling a bit off, though. Like, weird and uncomfortable, like a ship floating in a big blue sea," he laughed.

"Well, at least you're afloat, not drowning like in your dreams," he smiled. "This is all understandable, Brian. Why do you think you're feeling that way?"

Brian paused, "Huh?" He hadn't expected to be asked that. He paused for a second and said, "I guess it makes sense. I'm learning a new way of being, stepping into the unknown. I don't like how uncomfortable it is, it's stressful and I'm getting anxious some times."

"I understand. Be patient and gentle with yourself. It takes some time for the new thoughts and beliefs to take root. Know that it's normal to have some fear come up. Your old way is having a hard time and it's screaming so you don't let it go. Remember, you can choose."

Brian chuckled a bit too. "How long will it last?"

"It may take some time. With practice it'll get easier, trust me. Here's something to consider Brian: You're the tip of the arrow."

"Tip of the arrow?"

"Yes. There have been so many generations before you, on both sides of your family, see? For generations they've had challenges, some of the same ones you've had. You're the one putting the brakes on the years and years of momentum. Be proud of yourself for what you're up to. Celebrate what you're doing, Brian. You're a courageous man."

"It doesn't feel like that at times," he said.

"I know, Brian. I know. Trust. Have faith. Believe."

Brain took a deep breath. "When you explain it that way... it makes sense. In the moment though, it's well, in the words of a recent friend, 'It's freaky hard.'"

"Try and take comfort in the discomfort. You're growing, Brian. You're remembering who you are. It's like peeling an onion.

"During those times, consider taking a deep breath. Check your surroundings, ask yourself what day and time it is, along with where you are. This will help you get back to the moment. Tell yourself, 'Everything is ok. Everything will be okay.' This will help quiet your brain.

"Remember, sometimes your brain can't tell where or when you are, and above all, be gentle with yourself. If you need, imagine how you'd treat a kid going through what you are, and be that way with you."

Brian smiled. It all made sense.

"How come you know so much?"

The old man laughed, "Practice. Lots of practice with large splashes of compassion and patience." The old man paused and took a breath. "So, tell me about those doors that you closed."

Brian shared his decisions about not trying to convince Tammie to stay, of teaching and coaching, of officially ending things with Melinda.

"I'm not going to completely let go of coaching though. I'm going to continue and volunteer," Brian said.

The old man nodded and asked, "How did you feel afterwards, inside, after the decisions?"

"I felt a sense of relief. Not only like a weight was lifted, I felt cleaned out a bit, like there was room for something new. I think at that point I knew I was making the right choice. It was as if my body was agreeing with my choice."

"Good for you! No judgment and an inner knowing of what the right choice is for you. Kudos! Remember, allow yourself to have the feelings, Brian - feelings can be a key to life if you know what they are saying."

"Let the grief flow, too. If not, well, it'll keep you stuck. It can be like your car's in park and you just can't find the gear. If you're in it for more than a couple of days, that's a sign you're stuck. It's okay to ask for and get help, too.

"Well, I need to run. I have a schedule to keep, you know," and he started to get up.

"May I ask you one more question?"

"Besides that one?" the Old Man laughed.

"Yes, besides that one."

"Sure."

"How long will it take? How long will it take to create the life that I want?"

"Patience, Brian. There's a saying that goes: The map is not the territory."

"Huh?"

"The map is not the territory. It means, looking and focusing on where you're going is great, just don't forget to enjoy the journey. Have you noticed that once you get something, there's always something else you want."

"Yeah, now that you mention it. Yeah."

"So, enjoy your life and put a lid on your expectations. Expectations take you out of the present and, frankly, make us miserable inside."

"Thanks, Old Man."

"You bet. Well, I..."

They both said, in unison, "Have a schedule to keep," and laughed.

The old man made his way out of the deli and Brian felt right as rain. He felt hopeful, solid in the belief that he was on the right track, "his" track, to be exact.

Brian woke up the next day, energized and full of life. He took his run, had his breakfast, fired up his laptop and started applying to medical schools. A part of him couldn't believe what he was doing, it was a bit surreal, actually. It was as if he was a different person. The truth was, he was. He was the real, authentic, Brian. A smile crossed his face. The smile was really his, and from his inside, out.

As he went through the day, he decided he wanted to see the old man again. He went to the restaurant, nothing.

Second day, same thing. Nothing.

Third day, nothing.

A feeling of sadness came over him. He knew, deep down, that when he needed him, the old man showed up. In the meantime, he was ready for his new life. A life of purpose, of becoming a doctor, of helping children, finding his partner and being comfortable with himself once more.

Over the next few days, he noticed he was feeling uncomfortable again, it was pretty consistent. Frankly, things were so peaceful now that he was nervous. Brian wasn't used to things going so well.

He decided to accept it and let it be okay.

The next afternoon, he was in his deli having his usual: A turkey, ham and cheddar sandwich, a bag of chips and an orange soda.

He laughed, thinking again about how far he'd come, all the changes he'd made, and in walked the old man, smiling from ear to ear.

"You did it, Son. You did it!"

"I did what, Pops?"

"You found yourself! Many don't get this far, or even look for that matter. You have courage and an inner strength my boy. Most everyone has it, they just don't listen to their life. They ignore the call. All are chosen, really. Most just don't answer. You did, Brian, you did. Atta way, my boy!"

"Who are you?" he laughed.

"Does it matter, Brian, really?"

"No, I guess it doesn't. I do like your hat though."

"Me, too."

"As you go through your life, Brian, know that I'm always there for you. I want you to know there will be bumps along the way. You're human, so it's normal. When that happens, go back to what you know. Do what brings you peace, what centers and grounds you, and know I'll always be there for you… always."

"Gotta go!" The old man winked, smiled and slid out of the booth. He grabbed an orange soda, paid for it and opened the door to leave. He looked back at Brian and said. "I knew you had it in you, the whole time." He tipped his head in an affirming nod, smiled and left the deli.

Tears started to well up in Brian's eyes. He was on the road to becoming a doctor, he was going to help children lead happier and healthier lives. He would be doing what he loved - his purpose. He'd found it.

Everything was going to be okay.

More than okay.

Paul has over thirty years of experience in helping people better themselves. For twelve years, he served as a police officer and detective with the King County Sheriff's Department in Seattle, WA. In 1998, he drew upon his experience, rechanneled his efforts and created Peace Enforcement LLC. He has been working to positively impact the lives of adults, children, companies and people of all ages ever since.

Paul provides keynotes, breakouts, workshops, trainings and individual mentoring. Below is a partial list of the many ways he can lend a hand.

For Companies and Organizations:
>Workplace Improvement, Staff Development
>Management Skills, Leadership Training,
>Mentoring and more…

For Parents:
>Parent Workshops, Parent Retreats
>Presentations on numerous topics, including:
>>The Value of Positive Structure
>>Avoiding the Four Negative Parenting Styles
>>Is it You, or Is it Me? and more…

For Children and Young Adults:
>The Peace Enforcement Self Esteem Program
>Bullying Prevention, Where Did my Dreams Go?
>Positive Choices for a Happier Life
>The Language of Leadership and more…

For those that Work with Children:
>The Peace Enforcement Self Esteem Provider Program

For more information or to arrange to have Paul speak at your location or conference, contact us at:

Peace Enforcement LLC
206-650-5364
www.PaulFigueroa.com

* 9 7 8 0 6 9 2 9 9 6 4 8 5 *